Annotated Teacher's Edition

WRITE SOURCE
2000
SkillsBook
Editing and Proofreading Practice

. . . a resource of student activities
to accompany the
Write Source 2000 and
All Write handbooks

Level 7

WRITE SOURCE®

GREAT SOURCE EDUCATION GROUP
a Houghton Mifflin Company
Wilmington, Massachusetts

A Few Words About the
Write Source 2000 SkillsBook: Level 7

Before you begin . . .

The *SkillsBook* provides you with opportunities to practice the editing and proofreading skills presented in the *Write Source 2000* and *All Write* handbooks. The handbooks contain guidelines, examples, and models to help you complete your work in the *SkillsBook*.

Each *SkillsBook* activity includes a brief introduction to the topic and examples illustrating how to complete that activity. You will be directed to the page numbers in the handbook for additional information and examples. The "Proofreading Activities" focus on punctuation and the mechanics of writing. The "Sentence Activities" provide practice in sentence combining and in correcting common sentence problems. The "Language Activities" highlight each of the eight parts of speech.

The Next Step

Most activities include a **Next Step** at the end of the exercise. The purpose of the Next Step is to provide ideas for follow-up work that will help you apply what you have learned to your own writing.

> **Important Note:** If you are using this *SkillsBook* with the *All Write* handbook, refer to the handbook numbers at the bottom of each page. The numbers are printed in color.

Authors: Pat Sebranek and Dave Kemper

Printed in the United States of America

International Standard Book Number: 0-669-46777-4 (student edition)

 4 5 6 7 8 9 10 - POO - 04 03 02 01 00

International Standard Book Number: 0-669-46780-4 (teacher's edition)

 4 5 6 7 8 9 10 - POO - 04 03 02 01 00

Table of Contents

Proofreading Activities

Marking Punctuation

Editing for Mechanics

Using the Right Word

Sentence Activities

Language Activities

Nouns

Pronouns

Verbs

Adjectives

Adverbs

Adverbs	169
Forms of Adverbs	171
Double Negatives and Incorrect Usage	173

Prepositions

Prepositions	175

Interjections

Interjections	177

Conjunctions

Subordinating Conjunctions	179
Coordinating and Correlative Conjunctions	181

Parts of Speech

Parts of Speech Review 1 and 2	183

Proofreading Activities

Every activity in this section includes sentences that need to be checked for punctuation, mechanics, or correct word choices. Most of the activities also include helpful handbook references. In addition, the **Next Step** activities encourage follow-up practice of certain skills.

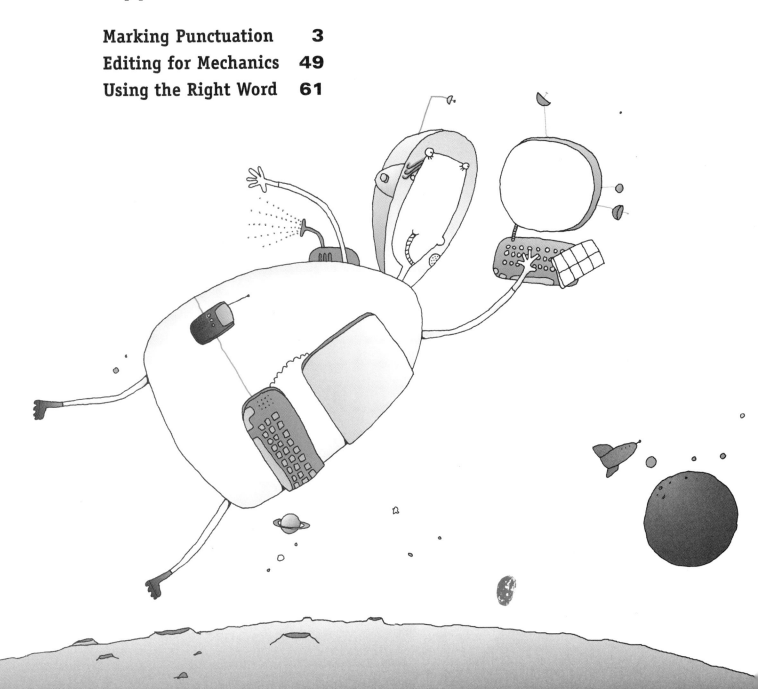

End Punctuation 1

Periods, exclamation points, and question marks are used to signal the end of a sentence. At the same time, the end punctuation marks tell the reader what kind of thought is being expressed in each sentence. (Turn to 387.1, 398.1-398.2, and 398.4 in *Write Source 2000* for more information.)

Directions   Put periods, question marks, and exclamation points where they are needed in the following paragraphs. Also supply the needed capital letters at the beginnings of sentences. The first sentence has been done for you.

1   Ants are amazing. *T*hey survived the extinction of the dinosaurs,

2   and now, millions of years later, there are more ants on the face of

3   the earth than any other creature.

4   The combined weight of all the ants in the world is about the

5   same as the combined weight of all living humans. *T*his is an incredible

6   fact since each ant weighs between 1 and 5 milligrams, or less than

7   one-millionth of a human's weight. *W*e are surrounded by 10 thousand

8   trillion of these creatures !

9   Ants are everywhere. *L*arge-eyed ants dominate the rain forest

10   canopy, while other ants live deep underground. *A*ggressive army ants

11   move in formation to hunt and devour animals in their paths. *S*ome

12   ants take slaves. *O*ther ants actually tame species, such as aphids, and

13   feed off their secretions.

All Write pp. 311-312

14   Ants prey upon and transport other insects and spiders into their

15 colonies, burying them and enriching the land. They move far more turf

16 than earthworms, mixing vast quantities of nutrients into the soil.

17   Harvester ants alter the environment by transporting seeds into

18 their nests for food. They decide which plants will succeed and which

19 will fail by tipping the balance in favor of the plants they prefer to eat.

20   Can you picture an ant gardening? Some ants create planting beds

21 out of soil, vegetable fibers, and other materials. Then they plant seeds

22 in the beds. As the plants grow, ants feed on them. The ant gardens of

23 Central and South America contain many plant species that cannot be

24 found anywhere else.

25   Two ant specialists, Bert Hölldobler and Edward Wilson, studied

26 ants for many years. They asked themselves if there might be a good

27 reason for the evolutionary success of ants. They concluded, "Ants, like

28 humans, succeed because they 'talk' so well."

29   Ants talk by releasing substances that have as much meaning for

30 other ants as words have for people. When ants in a colony

31 communicate, their companions cooperate instantly. Without the colony,

32 ants could not survive.

End Punctuation 2

Punctuation controls the movement of your writing. The end punctuation marks—periods, question marks, exclamation points—signal the end of a sentence and help the reader understand what you're trying to say in your writing. (Turn to 387.1, 398.1-398.2, and 398.4 in *Write Source 2000* for rules and examples.)

Directions   Place periods, question marks, and exclamation points where they are needed in the following narrative. Also, make sure the first word in each sentence is capitalized. The first two sentences have been done for you.

1   Because we had pulled in late the night before, we had to pitch

2   our tent in the dim light cast by our Coleman lanterns. We went

3   to bed with no idea where our campsite was located.

4   The next morning, my little brother and I were up as soon as the

5   birds began to chatter. We slipped on our clothes and shoes, unzipped

6   the screen door, and stepped outside. The others were still nestled in

7   their sleeping bags. To our surprise, 100 yards from our door lay a

8   small lake. It was a deep green, even in the morning haze. On closer

9   inspection, we saw that the lake was covered with a thick blanket of

10   algae. At the shoreline, we picked up some rocks and heaved them into

11   the water. Wherever they landed, large dark circles opened up and then

12   closed again.

13   The silence of the morning was broken only by the call of birds,

14   the dripping of trees, and the plops made by our high-arching rocks.

All Write pp. 311-312

15   Suddenly, we heard a tremendous splash along the shore. we

16 wheeled around. "look at that," my brother shouted. algae was splattered

17 over a 20-foot circle, and ripples were spreading fast.

18   "No fish could have done that," I said.

19   "Maybe a big turtle," my brother shouted.

20   "Or somebody threw a log," I said. "except nobody else is here."

21   "Could it be a sea serpent," my brother whispered.

22   "There are no such things," I chided him.

23   "Oh no, then what is that," he pointed to a line of humps moving

24 in the water far across the lake. i saw them, too. they moved, then

25 disappeared, then reappeared, and then disappeared again.

26   I wanted to believe in creatures like the Loch Ness monster. why

27 not, my little brother believed with all his heart. but I felt too old for

28 that. I thought about schools of fish, diving birds, wheels falling from

29 airplanes, meteors from outer space—scientific sorts of things.

30   What made the splash, I'll never know. but my brother and I will

31 never grow tired of telling the story of the monster in the lagoon—an

32 unsolved mystery in the annals of our family camping trips.

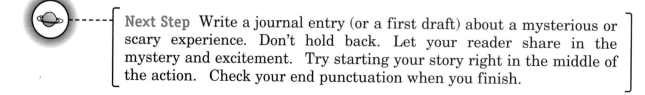

Next Step Write a journal entry (or a first draft) about a mysterious or scary experience. Don't hold back. Let your reader share in the mystery and excitement. Try starting your story right in the middle of the action. Check your end punctuation when you finish.

Punctuating Dialogue

Talking is so easy that you don't have to think about it. You just . . . talk. But recording "talk" on paper is another matter entirely—one that can be a lot of work. There are definite rules to follow regarding the use of quotation marks, commas, end marks, and capital letters. (Turn to 390.1, 399.1-399.3, and 400.1 in *Write Source 2000* for more information.)

EXAMPLE

"When will we leave for camp?" asked Todd.
(The *question mark* is placed inside the quotation marks because the quotation is a question.)

Directions   Punctuate the following dialogue with quotation marks, commas, and end marks. The first sentence has been done for you.

1   "All aboard, Scouts!" said Counselor Dave as he climbed into the

2   bus. "Are you men prepared to camp in the Sonora Desert tonight?"

3   "Not yet, Dave," shouted Andy. "We still need to buy some sandpaper!"

4   "Why do you need sandpaper?" asked the puzzled counselor.

5   Andy grinned. "We're going to need a map when we drive through

6   the desert."

7   As the bus pulled up to the campground, Counselor Dave shouted,

8   "The last man off this bus is a rotten egg!"

9   "Excuse me, Counselor," said Andy. "I can't get down off the bus."

10   "Why not?" asked the counselor. "What is the problem?"

11   "Everyone knows you can only get *down* from a goose," Andy

12   laughed.

All Write pp. 314 and 323-324

13   The next morning Counselor Dave rubbed his aching back and

14   yawned. I didn't sleep a wink in my tent, so I traded with Counselor

15   Ted. His tent wasn't any better.

16   Andy laughed and said, No wonder. You were just too tense, trying

17   to sleep in two tents.

_____

_____

_____

_____

_____

_____

_____

_____

_____

_____

_____

_____

Next Step In the space above, write a short dialogue with a partner. Take turns writing, just as if you were talking.

Comma Rules

Of all of the punctuation marks, the one that has the most uses—and probably causes the most confusion—is the comma. Your handbook covers 14 different rules for using commas. (Turn to 389.1-392.2 in *Write Source 2000* for more information.)

| **Directions** | Place commas correctly in each sample sentence. Then write the rule that applies to the comma usage. Use your handbook to do this exercise. The first sentence has been done for you. |

1. My favorite foods are hamburgers, french fries, and pizza.

Rule: Commas are used between words, phrases, or clauses in a series.

2. Mom must have told me at least 1,0 0 0,0 0 1 times to improve my diet.

Rule: Commas are used to distinguish hundreds, thousands, millions, and so on, in numbers.

3. On February 1, 2000, we will be moving to Boston, Massachusetts.

Rule: Commas are used to distinguish items in a date and items in an address.

4. "I'm sure," said Dad, "that Boston has some good pizza parlors."

Rule: Commas are used to set off the exact words of the speaker from the rest of the sentence.

5. We can't, however, stay very long.

Rule: Commas are used to set off a word, phrase, or clause that interrupts the main thought of a sentence.

All Write pp. 313-318

6. Yes‸ we'll be there on time.

Rule: Commas are used to separate an interjection or a weak

exclamation from the rest of the sentence.

7. Dad‸ is that all you think I'm worried about?

Rule: Commas are used to separate a noun of direct address from

the rest of the sentence.

8. The two friends love to go golfing‸ and they are working to qualify for

the state tournament next year.

Rule: A comma may be used between two independent clauses that

are joined by a coordinating conjunction.

9. My uncle beamed as he took hold of the large‸ shining trophy.

Rule: Commas are used to separate two or more adjectives that

equally modify the same noun.

10. My uncle‸ an expert angler‸ won the fishing contest.

Rule: Commas should separate an explanatory phrase (or a

nonrestrictive appositive) from the rest of the sentence.

11. Uncle Josh‸ who had traveled 600 miles to participate‸ was very glad he

had entered the fishing contest.

Rule: Commas are used to punctuate nonrestrictive phrases and

clauses (those phrases or clauses that are not necessary to the

basic meaning of the sentence).

Commas in a Series 1

Commas keep words and ideas from running together in a sentence. They are used between words, phrases, or clauses when there are three or more in a series. Read the following poem aloud.

Without a comma at my command, more
     punctuation I would demand.
There'd be no brake to slow the rush, of cursor,
     crayon, pen, or brush.
My days of writing soon would end, without that
     modest little friend
Who slips quietly in between, the words in series long or lean.

Now read it again to figure out where the missing commas should go. (Turn to 389.1 in *Write Source 2000* for more information.)

Directions   **Add commas to the series in the sentences below. The first sentence has been done for you.**

1. As we look back on the twentieth century, we should remember, think about, and try to learn from the events that shaped this remarkable period in history.

2. The United States fought in many conflicts during the twentieth century—among them World War I, World War II, the Korean conflict, and the war in Vietnam.

3. Imagine life without antibiotics to fight infections, vaccinations to prevent diseases, or scanners to diagnose our ailments.

4. In 1901, a visitor to a foreign city would have experienced strange new foods, clothing, and languages.

   All Write p. 313

5. Today, in large cities throughout the world, you can find not only the native foods, dress, and language but also McDonald's hamburgers, Levi jeans, and the English language.

6. Do you think that your interests, expectations, fears, beliefs, and desires are formed partly by television, music, and movies?

7. Some countries try to ban foreign entertainment, censor radio and television broadcasts, destroy historical records, or jail dissenting citizens in an attempt to control people's thoughts.

8. A history of the twentieth century will cover such topics as climate cycles, population growth, and urban sprawl.

9. People in the twentieth century created computers, radar, and penicillin, but they also gave the world hula hoops and Styrofoam cups.

10. In the first 25 years after the space age began, people orbited Earth, astronauts walked on the moon, and space probes studied the solar system.

11. When people study the last decade of the twentieth century, will they include baggy pants, nose rings, and colored hair as fads or major trends?

Next Step Choose the names of three of your classmates. Write two sentences including all three names. In the first sentence, use just the names themselves in a series. In the second sentence, include each of the names in a phrase or a clause about that person.

Commas in a Series 2

Commas keep words, phrases, and clauses in a series from running together. Understanding how to use commas is one of the best writing skills you can master. (For more information, turn to 389.1 in *Write Source 2000.*)

> **Directions**   **Add commas to the following sentences. Then label the parts of the sentence you've punctuated by writing *W* for word, *P* for phrase, or *C* for clause. The first sentence has been done for you.**

1. The U.S. National Park Service exists to protect places of special
            W   *W*   *W*   *W*
    historical*,* cultural*,* scientific*,* or recreational interest.
        P

2. Kill Devil Hill (site of the Wright brothers' first flight)*,* Manzanar
               P
    National Historic Site (where Japanese Americans were held during
                                        P
    World War II)*,* and Cumberland National Historical Park (site of the
    Warrior's Path across the Appalachian Mountains) commemorate events
    in our nation's history.

3. Recreational parks, like Wolf Trap Farm Park for the Performing Arts,
             W   *W*   *W*
    offer art*,* music*,* and theater in a natural, outdoor setting.

4.   *W*   *W*   *W*   *W*
    Yellowstone*,* Glacier*,* Yosemite*,* and Acadia National Parks protect complex
    ecosystems that might otherwise be lost forever.

5. The increasing number of visitors places great demands on the parks,
                   P   *P*
    causing destruction of plant life*,* disruption of animal habitats*,* and
            P
    pollution of waterways.

6. Even the largest national parks cannot exist as islands in a sea of
        W   *W*   *W*
    houses*,* roads*,* and automobiles.

All Write p. 313

7. Some parks require thousands of acres because elk herds need to migrate $\overset{C}{}$ from summer to winter pastures$\overset{C}{\underset{,}{\wedge}}$wolves need to range over large territories to support their packs$\overset{C}{\underset{,}{\wedge}}$and waterfowl need to move freely from one food source to another.

8. The Wilderness Act of 1964 is helping to save our parks by protecting $\overset{P}{}$ primitive areas$\overset{P}{\underset{,}{\wedge}}$re-creating natural habitat$\overset{P}{\underset{,}{\wedge}}$and banning development.

> **Directions** Now it's your turn: Write a paragraph about a park or recreational area you have visited or heard about. Be sure to share what makes the place unique. Include at least one sentence with a series of words, phrases, or clauses.

_____

_____

_____

_____

_____

_____

_____

_____

_____

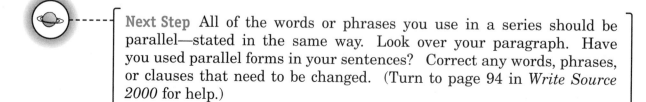

Next Step All of the words or phrases you use in a series should be parallel—stated in the same way. Look over your paragraph. Have you used parallel forms in your sentences? Correct any words, phrases, or clauses that need to be changed. (Turn to page 94 in _Write Source 2000_ for help.)

Other Comma Uses 1

If you want your writing to be clear and easy to understand, you will need to know how to use commas correctly. This activity will help you master three comma uses. (Turn to 389.1-389.3 in *Write Source 2000* for more information.)

EXAMPLES

Commas Separate Items in a Series:
Michael Jordan, Scottie Pippen, and Tony Kukoc started for the Chicago Bulls in the 1997-98 championship season.

Commas Separate Units in a Number:
The Bulls had a sellout streak of 530 games at the *21,500*-seat United Center.

Commas Separate Items in an Address or a Date:
On *January 30, 1998,* I watched the Bulls win at the United Center, which is located at *1901 W. Madison Street, Chicago, Illinois*.

Directions Using the rules described above as your guide, add commas as needed to the following sentences.

1. Scottie Pippen overcame back pain, a foot injury, and contract disputes to play an important part in the Bulls' sixth championship.

2. Scottie Pippen broke Magic Johnson's record of 1,724 all-time steals on February 21, 1998.

3. Michael Jordan collected 23 points, 8 assists, 6 rebounds, and 3 steals in the All-Star Game.

4. Michael Jordan was named NBA Player of the Week for the weeks of April 5, November 23, and December 21.

5. On February 12, 1999, we traveled to Chicago, Illinois, to see the Bulls' game against the Seattle Supersonics.

All Write p. 313

6. My brother, mother, and three sisters are all Seattle Supersonics fans.

7. That night, the Bulls shut down Sonics' players Vin Baker, Gary Payton, and Detlef Schrempf.

8. More than 21,000 fans attended the game and consumed 14,378 hot dogs, 10,910 bags of peanuts, and 18,345 soft drinks.

9. The Chicago Bulls will go down in history as one of the world's greatest teams after winning six championships in eight years.

10. Please mail your requests for NBA tickets to 240 Conastoga Street, Chicago Heights, Illinois 60411.

11. In 1998, Michael Jordan's annual salary was $33,000,000, the average NBA player made $2,600,000, and the minimum salary was $272,250.

12. In his first 13 seasons, Michael Jordan played 35,887 minutes in 930 games and scored 29,277 points.

13. Unlike the NFL, the NHL, and major league baseball, the NBA had never lost a regular season game because of a labor disagreement until the 1998-99 season.

14. You can contact the commissioner by writing him at the National Basketball Association, 645 Fifth Avenue, New York, New York 10022.

Next Step Write a paragraph of 5-6 sentences describing your favorite team—either a professional one or one of your local teams. Try to write some sentences using the rules for commas covered in this exercise. Share your paragraph with a classmate and check each other's work for the correct use of commas.

Other Comma Uses 2

Commas are like the dividers in your school binder. Just as a divider separates your math problems from your science notes, a comma helps you separate one clause or phrase from another, or one adjective from another. (For more information, turn to 391.2-391.4 in *Write Source 2000*.)

EXAMPLES

Commas Set Off Clauses:
Because Maria practices every day, she is a great snowboarder.
(*Because Maria practices every day* is a dependent clause.)

Commas Set Off Phrases:
To compete in the Olympics, Maria must train for years.
(*To compete in the Olympics* is an introductory phrase.)

Commas Separate Equal Adjectives:
Many *young, athletic* skiers are interested in snowboarding.
(The adjectives are "equal" because they could be written as *young and athletic*.)

Directions   Add commas as necessary to the following sentences. The first sentence has been done for you.

1. Because snowboarding is easy to learn, it is very popular.

2. Although snowboarding is sometimes compared to skateboarding, snowboarding is more like surfing.

3. Yesterday, the skiers struggled in the icy, rutted snow.

4. If you are interested in trying snowboarding, you should get the right equipment.

5. After testing out lots of boards, Karlowe decided to get a freestyle board.

6. Because it is the shortest and widest of snowboards, the freestyle board makes tricks easier to do.

All Write pp. 316-317

7. A *halfpipe* is a long, deep snow trench that snowboarders use to do flips and jumps.

8. Snowboards were invented by a creative East Coast surfer who got the idea by sliding over fresh, deep snow on a cafeteria tray.

9. Because snowboarders can get very wet and cold, they wear multiple layers of clothing.

10. Snowboarding can be done anywhere that skiing is done, except on flat cross-country trails.

11. Snowboarding equipment includes a freestyle or slalom board, bindings, and thick, chunky boots.

12. When first learning to snowboard, you have to decide to lead with your left foot or go goofy and lead with your right.

13. If you catch the front or rear edge of your snowboard too deeply in the snow, you may crash.

14. After finding a great place to board, just strap yourself to the board and surf down the hill.

15. If you are psyched to try snowboarding, you can rent some basic used equipment and ride the nearest halfpipe.

Next Step In a paragraph, describe why you like (or don't like) snowboarding. Try to use introductory phrases and clauses in your writing. Remember to separate each introductory phrase or clause from the rest of the sentence with a comma.

Commas Between Independent Clauses

One way to join two independent clauses is to connect them with a comma and a coordinating conjunction (*and, but, or, nor, for, so, yet*). Knowing that you can combine simple sentences in this way will help you to edit more effectively. Also, using this technique will help you to create smoother transitions and more interesting sentences. (Turn to 391.1 in *Write Source 2000* for more information.)

Directions   **Combine each of the following groups of sentences by using a comma and a coordinating conjunction. Avoid creating comma splices, which result from combining two sentences without a conjunction. The first sentence has been done for you.**

1. Blue whales are the largest living creatures. Human beings have the longest life span.

    Blue whales are the largest living creatures, but human beings have the

    longest life span.

2. Some swifts and falcons can travel at more than 200 miles per hour. Only hummingbirds can fly backward.

    Some swifts and falcons can travel at more than 200 miles per hour,

    but [(or) yet] only hummingbirds can fly backward.

3. Amazon ants are fierce. Fire ants are even fiercer and have been known to sting birds and other larger animals.

    Amazon ants are fierce, yet [(or) but] fire ants are even fiercer and

    have been known to sting birds and other larger animals.

4. Most mammals see color as shades of gray. Some apes and monkeys see all the colors.

    Most mammals see color as shades of gray, but [(or) yet] some

    apes and monkeys see all the colors.

All Write p. 316

5. A centipede should have 100 legs, according to its name. Some centipedes have more than 250 pairs of legs.

A centipede should have 100 legs, according to its name, yet some

centipedes have more than 250 pairs of legs.

6. Mammals have red blood. Insects have yellow blood.

Mammals have red blood, and insects have yellow blood.

7. Dogs can produce about 10 different sounds. Cats can produce more than 100 vocal sounds.

Dogs can produce about 10 different sounds, but cats can produce

more than 100 vocal sounds.

8. An owl cannot move its eyes. An owl must move its whole head to look in different directions.

An owl cannot move its eyes, so it must move its whole head to look

in different directions.

9. The house finch has spread rapidly. It has no natural predators.

The house finch has spread rapidly, for it has no natural predators.

10. Elephant seals can stay underwater for 30 minutes. They can dive to depths of more than 500 feet.

Elephant seals can stay underwater for 30 minutes, and they can

dive to depths of more than 500 feet.

Next Step Write a paragraph about a particular type of plant or animal that interests you. Try to use several compound sentences in your writing. Share your paragraph with a classmate.

Commas with Explanatory Phrases and Appositives

Commas are used to set off explanatory phrases from the rest of the sentence. Explanatory, or nonrestrictive, phrases contain information that is *not* necessary to the basic meaning of the sentence. That's why they are set off by commas. (For more information, see sections 391.4, 392.1, and 392.2 in *Write Source 2000*.)

EXAMPLES

Commas Set Off Explanatory Phrases:
The Grand Canyon, *located in northwestern Arizona,* is an incredible place.

Commas Set Off Nonrestrictive Appositive Phrases:
Bob, *my classmate,* visited the Grand Canyon.

Directions   Add commas to the following sentences as needed. The first sentence has been done for you.

1. Bob and Paola, Bob's neighbor, took a trip to the Grand Canyon last summer.

2. The Grand Canyon, which contains buttes, mesas, and valleys, is an awesome place to visit.

3. The boys rented burros, small donkeys, to use when traveling down the trails to the bottom of the canyon.

4. Their guide, Raoul, warned them that they should dress in layers because the temperature changes quickly in the canyon.

5. The temperature at the bottom of the canyon, even in the wintertime, is very hot.

All Write pp. 317-318

6. The two friends, both camping fanatics, wanted to set up camp at the bottom of the canyon.

7. They carried supplies, including tents and sleeping bags, on the backs of their burros.

8. Bob's parents, Phil and Maria Magrath, stayed at the top of the canyon.

9. The parents agreed, after a lot of persuading, to let the boys camp in the canyon alone.

10. The camping trip, four days and three nights, was one the boys will never forget.

11. The boys left from the canyon's south rim, 7,000 feet above sea level, and rode their burros down the steep trail.

12. The burros, named Pancho and Cisco, were very surefooted on the narrow trail that wound 5,000 feet down to the Colorado River.

13. The boys had to ride their burros very close together, and sometimes the burros, stopping to eat, stepped right near the edge of the trail.

14. Temperatures reached 100° F, which is 38° C, so the boys had to drink a gallon of water each day to avoid dehydrating.

15. The boys were on the lookout for a special type of rattlesnake, the Grand Canyon pink rattlesnake, that blends into the canyon's pink sandstone.

Next Step Think about a park or campsite that you know well, and imagine camping there with a friend. Then write a paragraph or two describing your experience. Ask a classmate to check your writing for correct comma usage. Then share your writing with the class.

Commas with Nonrestrictive Phrases and Clauses 1

Let's practice punctuating **nonrestrictive** phrases and clauses, including appositives. The first step is to identify the phrase or clause as nonrestrictive—or unnecessary to the basic meaning of the sentence. The next step is to set off the nonrestrictive phrase or clause with commas. (Review the differences between restrictive and nonrestrictive below and also see 391.4 - 392.2 in *Write Source 2000.*)

EXAMPLES

Restrictive:
The man *who made Silly Putty* became a millionaire.
(The information in the clause "who made Silly Putty" is needed to understand the sentence.)

Nonrestrictive:
Silly Putty, *a glob of stretchy goo,* was first called Gupp.
(The information in the phrase "a glob of stretchy goo" is not needed to understand the sentence.)

Directions   Add commas as necessary to the following sentences. The first sentence has been done for you.

1. Silly Putty, originally known as Gupp, was discovered in 1944 by James Wright.

2. James Wright, an engineer for General Electric, accidentally made Gupp in his laboratory.

3. James Wright thought that Gupp, which is made of boric acid and silicone oil, had no practical uses.

4. Peter Hodgson, an unemployed advertiser, found Gupp in a toy store.

All Write pp. 317-318

5. Hodgson called it Silly Putty and put it into small, plastic eggs that he sold for a dollar each.

6. The product that no one wanted made Hodgson a millionaire.

7. Silly Putty‸which became popular in the 1950s‸was pressed against comics and then stretched to make crazy impressions.

8. Soon kids who owned this stretchy goo realized that Silly Putty could also bounce very high.

9. In 1968, the astronauts who traveled on Apollo 8 carried Silly Putty into space to fight boredom and to fasten down tools during weightlessness.

10. In 1990, Binney and Smith Inc.‸the makers of Silly Putty‸added fluorescent colors.

11. Silly Putty‸which is now 45 years old‸is still a very popular toy.

12. A person who has a great imagination can think of new uses for ordinary products.

13. The Columbus Zoo‸which is in Ohio‸used Silly Putty to make plaster casts of gorillas' hands and feet.

Next Step Copy three sentences from this activity that contain a nonrestrictive phrase or clause. Then revise each sentence by crossing out the phrase or clause and substituting your own words. Be sure that the phrase or clause you add is nonrestrictive. Share your writing with a classmate.

Commas with Nonrestrictive Phrases and Clauses 2

Let's try punctuating more sentences that include restrictive and nonrestrictive information. Remember that nonrestrictive or unnecessary phrases and clauses are set off with commas, but restrictive phrases and clauses are not set off with commas. (For more information, turn to 391.4-392.2 in *Write Source 2000*.)

| **Directions** | Add a comma before and after the nonrestrictive information. (Not all sentences need commas.) The first sentence has been done for you. |

1. My youngest brother, Arturo, has a pet iguana named Felix.

2. Kids who want exotic pets must spend a lot of time learning how to take care of them.

3. Samir's parrot, Maurice, loves to mimic phone conversations and country singers.

4. The iguana that Joe owns eats both plants and animals.

5. The scarlet macaw, a popular pet, gets sick easily.

6. Cockatoos that mimic human speech are popular cage birds.

7. One of the largest cockatoos, the great palm, has black feathers and patches of bright red skin on its cheeks.

8. All cockatoos have feathered crests, which they can raise or flatten.

9. The tarantula, a long-legged, hairy spider, is found in warm areas.

10. Tarantulas use their big fangs to shoot venom, which can be deadly, into their victims.

All Write pp. 317-318

11. The miniature potbellied pig‸one of the smartest exotic pets‸is easy to train.

12. Pigs that wallow in the mud are trying to stay cool and to protect themselves from lice and other bugs.

13. The anaconda‸a semiaquatic snake‸is found in Central America and South America.

14. Anacondas‸which eat birds and small animals‸make unusual pets.

15. The giant anaconda that lives in our zoo is already 35 years old.

16. Levi wants to buy the boa that he saw advertised in the classified ads.

17. His mother‸who is afraid of snakes‸wants him to buy a macaw.

18. Most lizards‸except the desert iguana‸sleep during the hottest part of the day.

19. Exotic pets that are well cared for may live for many years.

20. Every year veterinarians must find new homes for exotic pets that have become too big or too dangerous for their owners.

21. Kids who want exotic pets must remember that these pets require a lot of care.

22. Owning an anaconda or a black widow spider‸both dangerous animals‸is not a good idea.

Next Step Write three sentences that contain nonrestrictive information. Ask a classmate to place the commas in the correct places. Try to stump your classmate with creative sentences.

Commas with Interruptions, Interjections, and Direct Address

Commas sometimes separate the unnecessary parts of sentences from the necessary parts. For example, when a word or phrase or clause is not necessary to the basic meaning of a sentence, that word or phrase or clause is separated from the rest of the sentence by a comma or by commas. **Interruptions, interjections,** or **nouns of direct address** are considered nonessential and are separated from the main sentence with commas. (For more information, turn to 390.2-390.4 and 391.4 in *Write Source 2000.*)

EXAMPLES

"Didn't you swim with dolphins, *Hillary?*"
"*Yeah,* I also swam near a shark, *believe it or not,* off the Florida Keys."

Directions   Add commas wherever they are needed in the sentences that follow. The first sentence has been done for you.

1. Of course, just the thought of a shark, as we all know, sends shivers down most swimmers' spines.

2. Contrary to popular belief, though, sharks rarely attack people.

3. "Simply stated, Bill, humans have not swum in the oceans long enough for sharks to adapt to hunting humans."

4. Many myths, most of them untrue, have developed about sharks.

5. Some people think, even though it's not true, that sharks must swim continuously to remain buoyant.

All Write pp. 314-315 and 317

6. Not surprisingly, this belief is based on the fact that, unlike other fish, sharks do not have a swim bladder filled with air to help them stay afloat in the water.

7. A shark's huge liver, almost 75 percent of its body weight, contains enough fat to make the fish float.

8. Without a fish's air-filled swim bladder, you see, deepwater sharks can move rapidly from the depths to the surface without decompressing.

9. Sharks, unchanged in the last 70 million years, are seldom seen in fossils.

10. Fossils are rare, unfortunately, because sharks have skeletons made of cartilage, like the framework of your nose and ears, instead of bone.

11. Some baby sharks are born live while others hatch from eggs deposited in pods known, believe it or not, as "mermaids' purses."

12. Just imagine, sharks must grow for about 15 years before they are mature enough to reproduce.

13. "Yes, Jamal, sharks need protection since they are being killed more quickly than they can replace themselves."

Next Step Write a letter to send to your local newspaper, or to share with your class, about a topic you know or care about. Remember to check your facts before sending or sharing your letter.

Comma Review

After reviewing the comma rules in the previous exercises, place commas correctly in the following sentences. (Turn to 389.1-392.2 in *Write Source 2000* for more information.)

1. A group of geese is a *gaggle*, but it is more commonly called a flock.

2. A *clip joint* is a shop, store, bar, or other place of business where customers are overcharged.

3. *Acrophobia* is the fear of heights, *claustrophobia* is the fear of enclosed spaces, and *hydrophobia* is the fear of water.

4. Abraham Lincoln was born on February 12, 1809, on a farm near Hodgenville, Kentucky.

5. Mr. Lincoln served as president of the United States from March 4, 1861, to April 15, 1865.

6. On June 3, 1979, more than 6, 8 5 0, 0 0 0 tons of oil spilled from an oil well in the Gulf of Mexico.

7. Mark's new address is 310 Greens Drive, Boston, Massachusetts 02109.

8. Send your requests to the *Daily Post*, 211 Main Street, Willowlane, Missouri 64402.

9. "Did you know," asked Dan, "that London Bridge is no longer in London?"

10. "Sue, these are my parents."

11. Mr. Dobson, our English teacher, is out with the flu.

12. Sliding into first base, I scraped my elbow raw.

All Write pp. 313-318

| Directions | Place commas correctly in the following sentences. (Refer to sections 389.1-392.2 in *Write Source 2000* if necessary.) |

1. "Dad, here are the good seats we've been telling you about."

2. "Wow," said Chris, "these are great!"

3. The usher, a young man with a beard, heard him and smiled.

4. Dad took orders and went to get sodas, popcorn, and pretzels.

5. The attendance, by the way, turned out to be more than 4 2,0 0 0.

6. The names and locations of Caroline Adams, M.D., and Samuel Cline, M.D., were posted on signs near the stage in case of emergencies.

7. We saw Miss Daniels, our neighbor, at the concert.

8. The music, which sounded perfect from our seats, carried out to the far ends of the stadium.

9. The concert was fantastic, and the crowd, loving it, clapped and screamed loudly.

10. Boy, it was hard to believe I would enjoy the same music as my dad, a child of the '60s.

11. For a bunch of old guys, the band called the Rolling Stones really rocked.

12. Everybody loved it when Mick Jagger, the Stones' lead singer, strutted across the stage.

13. The Stones' encore included "Paint It Black," "Angie," and "Under My Thumb," but they didn't play "Ruby Tuesday."

14. "This concert was a lot mellower than the Stones' concert at Altamont on December 6, 1969," Dad said.

Semicolons and Colons

A **semicolon** is sometimes used in place of a period or in place of a comma and a conjunction. A semicolon signals that the ideas in the two independent clauses are similar in thought or in style. (*He came; he conquered.*)

A **colon,** on the other hand, mainly calls the readers' attention to what comes after the colon, whether it be a list or a key word. (For more information, refer to 393.1-394.5 in *Write Source 2000.*)

EXAMPLES

Semicolons Join Independent Clauses:
My brother listens to punk rock; I listen to country music.
(Instead of a comma and a conjunction, a semicolon joins the two independent clauses.)

Semicolons Join Independent Clauses Connected by a Conjunctive Adverb:
Margarita listens to the Beatles; *however,* **she also likes jazz music.**
(A semicolon joins the two independent clauses with the conjunctive adverb *however.*)

Colons Introduce a List:
Motown Records has recorded many great artists: Stevie Wonder, Diana Ross, Smokie Robinson, the Temptations, and the Four Tops.

Colons Separate a Word for Emphasis:
Most record companies are motivated by the same thing: *money.*

Directions   Add semicolons and colons to the following sentences as needed. The first sentence has been done for you.

1. My friends and I want to start our own band; however, we can't agree on a name for it.

2. I think the name Purple Watermelons is cool; Yuri thinks that it's too weird.

3. Our band wants to get some experience playing in public; as a result, we're willing to play anywhere.

All Write pp. 319-320

4. We play many different kinds of music ;̂ however, we don't play anything very well.

5. My mom thinks there's only one word to describe our band :̂ loud.

6. Umberto plays the following instruments :̂ saxophone, guitar, trumpet, electric bass, synthesizer, and drums.

7. Last week we played at the Summerdale Senior Center ;̂ they didn't like our music.

8. We try to play all kinds of music :̂ folk, punk, rap, and country.

9. There is one thing that separates good bands from poor ones :̂ practice.

10. My friends and I dream of recording a hit song ;̂ we want to be big stars.

11. We practice in our garage ;̂ many famous musicians started out by playing in unique places :̂ garages, attics, churches, and parks.

12. We experiment with new styles ;̂ we have a country-pop song, a folk-punk song, and a swing-rock song.

13. Our best gig so far was the kindergarten graduation ;̂ we really had those kids rocking.

14. If we do become stars, there are many things I want to do :̂ buy a car, meet other stars, and get our band's picture on the cover of *Rolling Stone*.

15. We even have the title of our first album picked out :̂ *Fame*.

Next Step Write a paragraph about a dream you have for your future—what you hope to do when you are an adult. Describe that dream in a paragraph using the rules for semicolons and colons. Share your writing with a classmate.

Hyphens

Hyphens can be used to divide words and to form compound words. It might seem that hyphens have two opposite purposes; but really, hyphens have a single purpose: to make your writing clearer. (Refer to sections 396.1-397.3 in your *Write Source 2000* handbook for more information.)

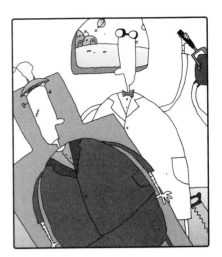

EXAMPLES

To Create New Words:
The *self-taught* musician started his own band.

To Make a Compound Word:
My *thirteen-year-old* sister is very good at Frisbee golf.

To Join Letters and Words:
The boomerang, a *V-shaped* stick, was sold by *Wham-O* Manufacturing.

Between Numbers in a Fraction or a Compound Number:
Why would *twenty-two* people each drink less than *one-half* cup of eggnog?

Directions   Add hyphens to the following sentences as needed. The first sentence has been done for you.

1. My brother-in-law owns nine Frisbees and thirty-two hula hoops.

2. My great-uncle was a friend of the Frisbee's inventors.

3. These self-employed inventors also created popular toys like boomerangs and slingshots.

4. Many ever-popular products were made by long-forgotten inventors.

5. The can opener was invented in 1858, but a more user-friendly version was made in 1870.

6. Blue jeans, the all-American pants, were invented by a canvas salesperson from San Francisco during the gold rush of the 1850s.

   All Write pp. 321-322

7. By inventing these basic all around pants, Levi Strauss created a new industry.

8. Blue jeans, now a world famous product, were first made out of canvas.

9. In 1916, an African American inventor was given a medal for his invention of the gas mask.

10. Use of the just invented gas mask saved the lives of three fourths of the workers in a tunnel explosion that year.

11. One of the ex directors of the American Red Cross was Dr. Charles Drew.

12. Out of work people sometimes become great inventors.

13. One of the most well known inventors was Alexander Graham Bell.

14. It took many years of trial and error research to invent the X ray machine.

15. By spilling some soft, sticky rubber on a red hot stove, Charles Goodyear created rubber as we know it today.

16. Forty one out of sixty eight people agreed that most inventions are made from one tenth inspiration and nine tenths perspiration.

17. If you have an idea for a super duper invention, you could possibly become a self made millionaire.

Next Step Invent a game that you could play with an everyday product found in your home. Then write a paragraph or two explaining how to play the game. Ask a classmate to read your writing and check for correct use of hyphens.

Dashes

Dashes set off parts of a sentence or show a sudden break in the flow of a sentence. They create pauses in your writing that are a bit stronger and more dramatic than comma pauses. Use them sparingly in formal writing. (Turn to 395.1-395.3 in *Write Source 2000* for more information.)

EXAMPLES

To Indicate a Sudden Break:
Never—and I mean never—has a toy sold as well as the hula hoop.

To Emphasize a Certain Word, a Series of Words, a Phrase, or a Clause:
The hula hoop—an Australian invention—was first sold in the United States.

To Indicate Interrupted Speech:
I wanted to tell you that—well, that—I lost your hula hoop.

Directions   Add dashes to the following sentences as needed. The first sentence has been done for you.

1. Both Frisbees and hula hoops were popular⌃very popular⌃in the 1950s.

2. Frisbees, Silly Putty, yo-yos⌃all of these have become classic toys.

3. The first hula hoops cost only $1.98⌃an unbelievable bargain!

4. Between 60 and 100 million hula hoops⌃an incredible number⌃were sold in just a few months.

5. Last week⌃no, let me see⌃was it⌃yes, last week⌃I bought a hula hoop.

6. The hula hoop was named after a very popular Hawaiian dance⌃the hula.

7. In the 1940s, students at Yale University tossed around pie platters from the local bakery⌃William R. Frisbie's Bakery⌃between classes.

8. The students were never⌃as you might imagine⌃given credit for their invention.

    All Write p. 322

Dashes and Hyphens

Dashes can add interruptions, information, or emphasis to your writing. Though dashes can be an effective writing tool, don't overuse them!

Hyphens connect words, numbers, and letters. (Turn to 395.1-395.3 and 396.1-397.3 in *Write Source 2000* for more about dashes and hyphens.)

EXAMPLES

Dashes:

Look out—that puddle is two feet deep!
(The dash and following text add emphasis and information to the warning.)

Hyphens:

Being a juggler isn't an average *nine-to-five* job.
(The hyphens turn the words *nine to five* into a single-thought adjective.)

Directions   **Punctuate the following sentences correctly. The first sentence has been done for you.**

1. That's not your run-of-the-mill slam dunk.

2. Your brother-in-law really knows how to fix cars.

3. My great-grandfather is 99 today.

4. There's only one sport—swimming—I've ever really enjoyed.

5. Make a U-turn so we can go back to that gas station.

6. No one—and I mean no one—may leave this room.

7. The woman slipped on the ice-covered sidewalk—an accident waiting to happen.

8. Arlo Hale is the president-elect of the Nottingham Running Club.

9. The blue-and-white-striped bench had a wet-paint sign on it.

10. I could eat only three-fourths of the big slice of strawberry-rhubarb pie.

Apostrophes 1

Apostrophes are used to form contractions and to show ownership or possession. (Turn to 402.1-403.4 in *Write Source 2000* for more information about apostrophes.)

EXAMPLES

To Form Contractions:
Wouldn't riding a one-wheel bicycle be fun?
(would + not = wouldn't)

To Show Possession:
A *unicycle's* wheel is small.

Directions For each of the underlined words below, write *C* if an apostrophe is used correctly, add apostrophes to the words that need them, and correct any misplaced apostrophes. The first two sentences have been done for you.

1 Paula loves to ride her friends' unicycle. She *C* didn't take

2 long to learn, and she doesn't worry about falling. A unicycle is

3 recognized easily by ~~it's~~ *its* single wheel. Paula's *C* friend received his unicycle

4 from his brother-in-law; its *C* seat is mounted on a pole 20 feet high.

5 Naturally, a ~~unicycles'~~ *unicycle's* pedals must be up near the seat. Paula's *C* friend's *C*

6 vehicle is not your usual, run-of-the-mill unicycle. Because pumping a

7 unicycle is hard, sweaty work, there's a fan installed on the 20-foot pole

8 with a generator attached to the wheel's *C* hub. Isn't Paula's *C* ~~friends'~~ *friend's*

9 riding machine a sight to see? Now they can't wait to try out the

10 ~~brother's-in-law~~ *brother-in-law's* new toy—a *miniature* unicycle.

All Write pp. 325-326

Apostrophes 2

By now, you know that apostrophes are used to form contractions and to show possession, but they can do other things, too. In this activity, you'll discover some other ways you can use apostrophes. (Turn to 402.1-402.4 in *Write Source 2000* for more information.)

EXAMPLES

To Form Plurals:
Be sure to cross your *t*'s and dot your *i*'s.

In Place of Omitted Letters or Numbers:
In the summer of '98, we rode 16 *rockin'* roller coasters.

To Express Time or Amount:
My dad took a *week's* vacation so that he could come with us.

Directions Add at least one apostrophe to each of the following sentences. You will need to form contractions in some sentences.

1. Marcel ~~could not~~ *couldn't* wait to ride the Rattler, the fastest wooden roller coaster in the world.

2. He saved a month's worth of allowance for the class of '99 trip.

3. The figure 8's on this roller coaster made it especially scary.

4. Lionel ~~does not~~ *doesn't* know whether he should try the Hercules or Batman.

5. It's hard to imagine that either could be scarier than the Desperado.

6. People sat in rows of 2's and 3's in the hanging roller coaster.

7. Tomorrow's rides will be even more amazing than today's rides.

8. ~~They will~~ *They'll* be faster, bigger, and more daring.

9. Who's going to be brave enough to try these new roller coasters?

 Next Step Write a journal entry (or a first draft of a story) about a special vehicle in your life. Make sure that you use apostrophes correctly in your writing. Share your results.

Apostrophes 3

Apostrophes can be used in your writing to show possession—to say, "Hey, that belongs to me!" (Turn to 402.5-403.4 in *Write Source 2000* for more details about how to use apostrophes to show possession.)

EXAMPLES

Singular Possessives:
Cedar Point's Mean Streak roller coaster is one of the world's longest wooden coasters.

Plural Possessives:
The *visitors'* hearts raced as they plunged down the coaster hills.

Shared Possession:
Latoya, Eli, and *Gabriel's* favorite roller coaster is the Wild Thing at Valleyfair. Latoya's, Eli's, and Gabriel's favorite snacks are different.

Possessives in Compound Nouns:
My *sister-in-law's* biggest fear is falling out of a roller coaster.

Possessives with Indefinite Pronouns:
Everyone's hands grab the safety bar during loops.

Directions   In the following sentences, add an apostrophe where needed to show possession. But be careful—not every sentence needs an apostrophe. The first sentence has been done for you.

1. The earliest roller coasters' tracks were made from cut lumber and tree trunks.

2. The first roller coasters were made in Russia in the fifteenth century.

3. Children's lives were often in danger on those early roller coasters.

4. The world's first hanging roller coaster appeared in 1981 in Cincinnati, Ohio.

5. The world's tallest and fastest hanging roller coaster is the Alpengeist.

6. The Alpengeist's fastest speed is 67 miles per hour.

All Write pp. 325-326

7. Its features include diving loops, rolls, and high-speed spirals.

8. My sister-in-law's scariest ride was on the Thunder Run at Kentucky's Six Flags.

9. Roller coasters' safety rules protect the lives of their passengers.

10. Jacco's, Ruth's, and Tobie's families spend the summer going from one amusement park to the next.

11. The world's first roller coaster to reach 100 miles per hour was Dreamworld's Tower of Terror.

12. Located at King's Island, the 7,400-foot Beast is the world's *(optional)* longest roller coaster.

13. The Beast, which is 20 years old, is everyone's favorite wooden roller coaster.

14. This year's most popular roller coaster was the Desperado at Buffalo Bill's Resort in Nevada.

15. The country's first steel roller coaster was Disneyland's Matterhorn Mountain, which opened in 1959.

16. Coney Island's Wonder Wheel combines a ferris wheel's circular path with a roller coaster's thrills.

17. Our family rated ten roller coasters, and my two brothers' top choice was Apollo's Chariot.

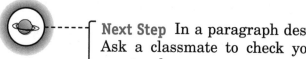

Next Step In a paragraph describe your favorite amusement park ride. Ask a classmate to check your writing for correct use of possessive apostrophes.

Italics and Quotation Marks

Quotation marks are used to punctuate titles of shorter works. Titles of longer works are italicized. (If you are handwriting the title of a longer work, you should underline it.) For more information about italics and quotation marks, refer to 399.1-400.3 and 401.1-401.5 in *Write Source 2000*.

Directions	Punctuate the following sentences. Remember that periods and commas are always placed inside quotation marks. The first sentence has been done for you.

1. In the Utne Reader magazine article "How to Future-Proof Your Life," the author says you should pack lightly.

2. A burglary at the Watergate Hotel in Washington, D.C., was reported in the Washington Post and chronicled in the book All the President's Men.

3. Two books I like are Are You My Mother? and The Cat in the Hat.

4. As Titanic sank, the band supposedly played "Nearer, My God, to Thee."

5. A stirring song, "The Circle of Life," from the movie The Lion King draws inspiration from African drumming.

6. On-line magazines, or interactive magazines, such as Hip Mama, appeal to readers who would rather surf the Internet than browse through libraries.

7. Melville's novel Moby Dick is famous for its whaling lore, such as the chapter titled "Scrimshander."

8. Anyone who has tried to buy something from a rude salesperson can appreciate Elaine's struggles in "The Soup Nazi," an episode of Seinfeld.

All Write pp. 323, 324, and 327

9. Please turn up the volume so we can hear the song "Octopus's Garden."

10. Our faithful retriever wouldn't bring in the newspaper because the banner headline read "Man Bites Dog."

11. In 1963, John Glenn blasted into space in Friendship 7, and 35 years later, he returned to space aboard the space shuttle Discovery.

12. Sherlock Holmes utters the classic line, "By Jove, Watson, I've got it!" in "The Adventure of Charles August Milverton," a story from the book The Return of Sherlock Holmes.

13. "Zoot Suit Riot" was a big hit for the Cherry Poppin' Daddies from their Zoot Suit Riot CD.

14. Many newspapers, including the New York Times, Chicago Tribune, and San Jose Mercury News, have their own Web sites.

15. Humphrey Bogart never said, "Play it again, Sam," in the movie Casablanca, a film based on a play called Everybody Comes to Rick's.

16. The school newspaper, the Yorkville Yacker, reviewed the movie Babe: A Pig in the City in an article entitled "Babe, a Real Oinker."

17. The musical group Chicago, the musical play Chicago, and the poem "Chicago" by Robert Frost are all named after the Illinois city.

Next Step On your own paper, write three sentences. In the first sentence, include the title of a song. In the second one, include the title of a poem, and in the third, include the title of an article in a newspaper. When you have finished, check your work to be sure you have used italics and quotation marks correctly.

Italics and Parentheses

Italics are like flashing lights. They catch your attention right away because they look different than the regular type on the page. Italics alert readers to titles, foreign words, and words that are being used in a special way.

Parentheses separate words or phrases added to a sentence to make it clearer. They are really a lot like commas and dashes because they help prevent ideas from getting jumbled together. We use parentheses instead of commas and dashes when we want less emphasis on the separated material. (*Write Source 2000* explains the uses of italics and parentheses in more detail in sections 395.4 and 401.1-401.5.)

EXAMPLES

Italics in Titles:
The River is one of my favorite adventure books.

Italics for Foreign Words:
Orcinus orca is the Latin name for killer whale.

Italics for Special Uses:
Try to say rubber baby buggy bumpers five times fast.

Parentheses for Added Information:
The author (Gary Paulsen) is a favorite of kids.

| Directions | Add underlining (for italics) or parentheses to the following sentences. The first sentence has been done for you. |

1. I have such a hard time saying the word <u>minimum</u>.

2. S. E. Hinton wrote <u>The Outsiders</u> when she was 16 years old.

3. The article on skydiving was in last month's issue of <u>Sports Illustrated</u>.

4. Our house in Grand Marais (actually the north shore of Lake Superior) is really a cabin.

5. This summer I saw <u>The Borrowers</u> at a movie theater downtown.

All Write p. 327

6. The Latin name for one of the largest dinosaurs is <u>Tyrannosaurus Rex</u>.

7. Everyone thought <u>Titanic</u> was an unsinkable ship.

8. The <u>New York Times</u> published an article about kids starting their own businesses.

9. What is the French word for <u>love</u>?

10. How many <u>i</u>'s are there in the word <u>Mississippi</u>?

11. You should order at least six dozen (72) barbecue buns for the party.

12. The tongue twister <u>Peter Piper</u> is harder to say than the tongue twister <u>she sells seashells</u>.

13. With his new braces, Paul found it hard to say <u>s</u>'s and <u>th</u>'s.

14. He rode his bike (actually a moped) back and forth to school.

15. Have you read <u>The Hatchet</u>, another book by Gary Paulsen?

16. If you switch the letters <u>r</u> and <u>d</u> in the word <u>read</u>, you get <u>dear</u>.

17. Parentheses (those curvy brackets) are always used in a pair to set off words in a sentence.

18. CD's (compact discs) replaced magnetic tapes as the main format for storing recorded music.

19. The Spanish word <u>hola</u> and the Italian phrase <u>buòn giorno</u> mean the same thing (hello).

Next Step Write a paragraph about your favorite book or movie. Describe it using details that would convince someone else to read or see the book or movie you are describing. What made that book or movie really interesting? Use italics and parentheses whenever necessary in this paragraph. Share your paragraph with the class.

Punctuation Review 1

Directions Proofread the paragraphs below. Draw a line through any mark of punctuation or word that is used incorrectly; add any needed punctuation or capital letters. (For more information turn to 387.1-403.4 in *Write Source 2000*.) The first two sentences have been done for you.

1   Picture a New England beach in autumn. The sky is clear, the

2   sun warms your face. The green sea has washed ashore almost 100 of

3   it's most magnificent creatures whales to die. A biologist walks among
     its

4   the bloating bodies of the whales, and he is clearly puzzled.

5   Mass whale suicides, or "strandings" as they are called, occur year

6   after year. Many people have tried to understand these unusual

7   suicides, even Aristotle, the ancient Greek, philosopher, thought about
                  E

8   the whales' deaths. Although he decided the whales may indeed be

9   killing themselves, modern biologists are not so easily convinced."

10   One researcher points out that the whales are descended from

11   land dwelling animals. He thinks the whales may simply be

12   remembering their ancient roots, and beaching themselves to "go home."

13   This habit, however, would have put the whale close to extinction years

14   ago, so the idea doesn't make much sense.

15   A newer theory suggests that the whales blindly follow their food

16   supplies, into shallow water. For example, they may swim after a shoal

17   of squid, quickly eat their dinner, and then find themselves too close to

18   the shore.

All Write pp. 311-327

19   Another theory says that whales follow the earth's magnetic forces

20   as though they were following a road map. the whales travel wherever

21   these forces lead. Unfortunately, the magnetic flow will sometimes cross

22   the shoreline and guide the whales along a collision course with the

23   beach.

24   Biologists realize, of course, that none of these findings are

25   complete explanations. Some feel that the strandings must have a

26   number of causes, not just one.

_____

_____

_____

_____

_____

_____

_____

_____

_____

Next Step In the space above, write freely for 3 to 5 minutes about punctuating writing. Consider what's easy or hard about it, what's important or confusing. Then, double-check your work by reviewing the punctuation rules and examples in your handbook.

Punctuation Review 2

Directions   Review rules 389.1-403.4 in your *Write Source 2000* handbook. These rules discuss commas, semicolons, colons, dashes, parentheses, hyphens, question marks, exclamation points, quotation marks, italics, and apostrophes. Then punctuate the following paragraphs correctly.

1   Famous celebrities pose for pictures, sign autographs, and make a

2   lot of money. Going unnoticed, however, are the other stars the animal

3   actors who work hard to keep these human celebrities in business. These

4   truly great stars are dogs like Timmy's Lassie and Marty Crane's Eddie

5   (on *Frasier*).

6   Lassie is probably the best-known television pet. However, the dog

7   we all now know as Lassie was not originally cast for the part. He

8   was hired instead as a stunt dog. Pal (Lassie's real name) was a

9   beautiful sable collie, and he was trained by Rudd Weatherwax, a

10 Hollywood dog trainer.

11   In one of the early filming sessions for the movie <u>Lassie Comes</u>

12 <u>Home</u>, Lassie needed to swim across a raging river, pull herself out of

13 the water, and lie on the bank pretending to be dead. The starring

14 dog who originally played the part of Lassie could not be convinced to

15 step into the water. So Pal, the stunt dog, was called into action. Pal

16 swam across the raging river—even the swirling rapids—without any

17 difficulty. He didn't even shake out his coat when he got to the other

18 side; he lay down and pretended to be dead. The original starring dog

19 was fired, and Pal was hired as the new Lassie.

20 Eddie, the terrier who stars on the TV show <u>Frasier</u>, is also a

21 show-stealing star. He is the talented dog who sometimes gets more

22 laughs than the show's human star, Kelsey Grammar. Eddie (whose

23 real name is Moose) does many comical tricks and makes goofy facial

24 expressions that make it seem as though he knows just what makes

25 an audience laugh. He has appeared on the covers of these popular

26 magazines: <u>Life</u>, <u>TV Guide</u>, and <u>Entertainment Weekly</u>.

27 Animal actors are so well trained that we often forget that they

28 can't be taught to act in the same way that humans are taught.

29 Today, with movies like <u>Air Bud</u> and <u>Bear</u>, animal films are even more

30 popular than ever. Thanks to the dedication of their trainers, the work

31 of their agents, and the talents of these incredible animals, we are able

32 to enjoy a whole new generation of animal films and TV shows.

Capitalization 1

Good writers write good sentences. They also check their details and proofread their work to get rid of errors. In this exercise, you will proofread your writing for capitalization errors. The key to capitalizing correctly is remembering to capitalize all proper nouns and proper adjectives. (Turn to 404.1-407.3 in *Write Source 2000* to review capitalization rules.)

EXAMPLES

Capitalize Historical Events and Proper Nouns:
The 1998 *Winter Olympics* were in *Nagano, Japan.*

Capitalize Particular Sections of the Country:
The *West Coast* is the perfect place for skiing and sledding competitions.

Capitalize Names and Words Used as Names:
Felix and *Aunt Necia* are going to the games in *Sydney, Australia.*

Capitalize Titles Used with Names:
For years, *President* Juan A. Samaranch has been in charge of the games.

Directions Add capital letters to the following sentences as needed. The first sentence has been done for you.

1. The *I*nternational *O*lympic *C*ommittee decides where the games will be held.

2. Nagano, *J*apan, was a perfect place for the winter games.

3. Winter conditions in *N*agano are ideal for skiing and skating.

4. The *J*apanese *A*lps surround *N*agano.

5. During the planning for the games, *G*overnor *G*oro *Y*oshimura met with the *J*apanese *O*lympic *C*ommittee.

6. The *S*nowlets were the official *O*lympic mascots of the *N*agano games.

7. The *S*nowlets' names were *S*ukki, *N*okki, *L*ekki, and *T*sukki.

All Write pp. 328-332

8. Officials from the j̵apanese government hoped that many tourists would
   come to the games.

9. In social studies, we studied the culture of j̵apan.

10. m̵r. m̵arkus, our science teacher, visited j̵apan last spring.

11. The ølympic flame was first used in the opening ceremonies in the 1936
    summer games in b̵erlin.

12. The ølympic flag has five rings that represent unity among the continents
    of ⱥfrica, the ⱥmericas, ⱥsia, ⱥustralia, and ėurope.

13. My uncle was at the competition where Nadia ȼomaneci, a ɍomanian
    gymnast, won the first perfect score in ølympic gymnastics.

14. The i̵nternational s̵ports f̵ederation decides the rules for gymnastic
    competitions.

15. World ẉar I forced the cancellation of the 1916 games, planned for b̵erlin,
    ǥermany.

16. At the 1936 b̵erlin games, ⱥfrican-ⱥmerican athlete j̵esse øwens won gold
    medals in the 100-meter dash, 200-meter dash, and the long jump event.

17. Last f̵riday, m̵ayor m̵iller and five council members attended an Olympic
    site-selection meeting in ȼhicago.

18. The meeting was sponsored by the f̵ord m̵otor ȼompany.

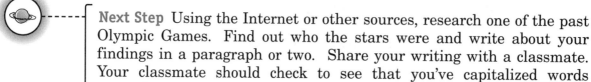

Next Step Using the Internet or other sources, research one of the past
Olympic Games. Find out who the stars were and write about your
findings in a paragraph or two. Share your writing with a classmate.
Your classmate should check to see that you've capitalized words
correctly.

Capitalization 2

Here's another exercise to help you to capitalize words correctly. Some helpful examples are given below. (Turn to 404.1-407.3 in *Write Source 2000* for more information and rules. Also refer to 409.4-409.6 for examples of how to capitalize abbreviations.)

EXAMPLES

Capitalize Titles, Days, and Months:
The History of Olympic Games will be available in our library *Friday, February* 19.

Capitalize Organizations and Abbreviations:
The *International Olympic Committee* is sometimes referred to as the *IOC*.

Capitalize the First Word at the Beginning of a Direct Quotation:
My friend Sasha said, "*Well*, my favorite Olympic sport is diving."

Directions — Add capital letters where necessary to the following sentences. The first sentence has been done for you.

1. The u.s.s.r. [U.S.S.R.] sent its first olympic [O] team to the games in helsinki [H], finland [F].

2. The encyclopaedia [E] britannica [B] has a large section on the olympic [O] games [G].

3. My teacher said that the russians [R] boycotted the games in los [L] angeles [A] because americans [A] boycotted the games in moscow [M].

4. Felix said, "the [T] winter games were held in nagano [N], japan [J], this year."

5. "I wish that I could have gone," he continued, "but it was too expensive."

6. "Well," I replied, "at least you got to watch the games on tv [TV]."

7. The ioc [IOC] has introduced some new sports to the olympics [O] in the last 10 years.

8. "the [T] number of women's sports has certainly increased," said Felicia.

9. my [M] uncle was a speed skater for the dutch [D] team in the 1994 olympics [O].

10. the [T] winter games were canceled in 1940 and 1944 because of world [W] war [W] II.

All Write pp. 328-332 and 335

11. Bonnie blair, a u.s. skater, won the 500- and 1000-meter speed-skating races
       B   *U.S.*

in 1994.

12. Is blade runner a book about olympic speed skating?
      B   *R*   *O*

13. sports illustrated features many articles about the international stars of the
  S   *I*

olympic games.
O   *G*

14. After watching the 1998 Winter Olympic Games, my friend Ross said, "like,
                                           L

Dude, those snowboarding events were awesome."

15. The IOC (International Olympic Committee) should not be confused with the
  IAC   *IBC*

iac (International Athletic Conference) or the ibc (International Bowling

Congress).

16. Each country that participated in the Olympic Games has a National
                                 NOC

Olympic Committee (noc) that helps select athletes for its teams.

17. The official Web site of the ioc is called the olympic movement, and it gives
                      IOC   *T* *O*   *M*

information about past, present, and future Olympic Games.

18. I remember my English teacher, mr. Oden, saying, "my favorite sports poem
                             M   *M*

is 'to an Athlete Dying Young' by A. E. Housman."
   T

Next Step Write an imaginary conversation between you and your
favorite Olympic or sports champion. Be sure to describe her or him
first so that we will know more about the star. Share your writing with
a classmate and ask her or him to correct any capitalization errors.

Abbreviations and Numbers

Using abbreviations is convenient, but if you overuse them or use them incorrectly, they can make your writing confusing.

Using numbers can be a bit tricky. The big question is whether you should write numbers out or use figures. The type of writing often determines your choice. In technical, scientific, and business writing, figures are often used. In general writing, however, numbers are more often spelled out. (For more information about numbers and abbreviations, see 387.3, 404.4, and 409.4 - 410.6 in *Write Source 2000*.)

EXAMPLES

Abbreviations:
Mr. and Mrs. James Wilkins Jr. are returning from their trip to Ethiopia.
(Acceptable)

They came home to the U.S. on Thurs., but they will return to Africa in Dec.
(Unacceptable: Do not abbreviate the names of states, countries, days, or months in formal writing.)

Numerals Only:
Please read pages 345-362 in chapter 3 for tomorrow.

Numerals in Compound Modifiers:
I asked for three 13-year-old volunteers.

Directions Correct any abbreviation or number error by drawing a line through the error and writing the correct form above it. Do not change any abbreviation or number that is used correctly.

1. *Twelve*
   ~~12~~ of Hugo's best friends came to visit him.

2. On May ~~six~~ *6*, Hugo and his friends celebrated his 10th birthday.

3. Last year, when Hugo turned nine, his parents bought him a new bike.

4. His father is a ~~prof.~~ *professor* who works for ~~nasa~~ *NASA*.

All Write pp. 329 and 335-337

5. His mother is an ~~m.d.~~ *M.D.* who specializes in ~~ER~~ *emergency room* medicine.

6. Now that he is going to be ~~ten,~~ *10* Hugo is hoping to get ~~3~~ *three* presents for his birthday.

7. Someday Hugo would like to work for the ~~cia~~ *CIA* or ~~fbi,~~ *FBI* so he wants a spy kit.

8. He would also like ~~2~~ *two* 250-piece sets of building blocks.

9. The gift he really hopes to receive is an IBM ~~pc.~~ *PC*

10. Hugo might have to wait for his ~~pc~~ *PC* because his parents are afraid of the year ~~two thousand,~~ *2000* or Y2K, computer problem.

11. His pal Joey gave Hugo a geode from ~~Tenn.,~~ *Tennessee* and his friend Jason gave him a wooden box from ~~Ark.~~ *Arkansas*

12. But the strangest gift Hugo received came from his dad's friend ~~Doctor~~ *Dr.* Burns, ~~PHD,~~ *Ph.D.* a ~~N.A.S.A.~~ *NASA* rocket scientist.

13. Dr. Burns gave Hugo a ~~twelve~~ *12*-ounce moon rock brought back on *Apollo 17,* which landed on the moon ~~Dec.~~ *December* 11, 1972.

14. Joey hung around, and he and Hugo watched ~~W.W.F.~~ *WWF* wrestling on the WB network and saw about 1 million commercials.

15. Joey's dad picked him up and drove down Highway ~~thirty-six~~ *36* back to their home.

16. Hugo had a great birthday, but his mom and dad were exhausted from having to deal with ~~13~~ *thirteen* 10-year-old boys from 10:30 ~~AM~~ *a.m. (A.M.)* to 7:00 ~~PM.~~ *p.m. (P.M.)*

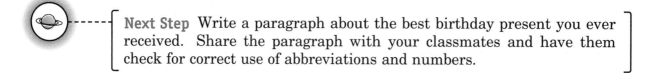

Next Step Write a paragraph about the best birthday present you ever received. Share the paragraph with your classmates and have them check for correct use of abbreviations and numbers.

Capitalization and Abbreviations Review

Attention to detail means different things to different people. To a writer it means carefully reviewing a final draft to make sure that every *i* is dotted, every *t* is crossed, and every capital letter is in place. (Turn to 387.3, 404.1-407.3, and 409.4-409.6 in *Write Source 2000* for more information on capitalization and abbreviations.)

Directions Put a line through any word or letter below that is capitalized or abbreviated incorrectly. Correct each error and add punctuation where needed.

1. home of mrs. goodwrench *(M G)*

2. The Mayor is going to speak Tues. *(m Tuesday.)*

3. Did you call me, uncle Jim? *(U)*

4. Go East until you come to the library. *(e)*

5. Isn't your Mother from the East? *(m)*

6. This humid august weather is unbearable. *(A)*

7. I heard mom calling for you, Dad. *(M)*

8. I've always liked History Courses. *(h c)* Are you taking history 201 next Fall? *(H f)*

9. Mr. Kipp let me read there's a bat in bunk five. *(T B / B F)*

10. Castles were quite common in the Middle ages. *(A)*

11. Are you going to take that job out west? *(W)*

12. No, I am going to take the job down South.

13. the Battle of Bunker Hill

14. She shouted, "don't touch the stove!" *(D)*

15. Navajo pottery, Dutch pastry, Chinese muslin

16. Have you read "by the waters of babylon"? *(B W / B)*

17. The Chicago Trib. is a fine daily newspaper. *(Tribune)*

18. Bill Clinton was once the governor of AR. *(Arkansas)*

19. "make room," barked the mover. *(M)* "This piano is heavy."

All Write pp. 328-332 and 335-336

20. J/ "jerome," yelled C/coach R/rogers, "stay back on defense!"

21. They'll put people on the P/Planet Mars.

22. lakes Michigan and Superior

23. Colorado R/river

24. T/the B/bailey M/middle S/school S/science C/club will sell refreshments.

25. Bob Madsen, m.d. *M.D.*

26. Mr. Jackson, M/mark's father, joined the staff at Trinity H/hospital.

27. Kellogg's C/crispix cereal

28. the F/first A/amendment to the C/constitution of the U-S-A *United States of America*

29. He's busy with his American History 212 assignment.

30. Hawaii is in the Pacific O/ocean.

Directions   Supply the necessary capital letters in the following narrative. (There are 49 capital letters needed.)

1   A/america's best-loved radio program, A/a P/prairie H/home C/companion, left the

2   air on J/june 13, 1987, at the height of its popularity.   B/broadcast from the

3   W/world T/theater in S/st. P/paul, M/minnesota, the show charmed millions of listeners.

4   H/host G/garrison K/keillor took his audience into the heart and soul of an

5   imaginary town in M/minnesota called L/lake W/wobegon—also known by the

6   following title: "T/the T/town T/that T/time F/forgot and the D/decades C/could N/not

7   improve." W/who could ever forget F/father E/emil, O/our L/lady of P/perpetual

8   R/responsibility, the S/sidetrack T/tap, B/bertha's K/kitty B/boutique, P/powdermilk

9   B/biscuits, R/ralph's P/pretty G/good G/grocery, and "T/the S/statue of the U/unknown

10   N/norwegian"?   After several years, the show returned to the airwaves due to

11   popular demand.

Capitalization Mixed Review

Directions   Carefully read the following essay and add capital letters wherever necessary. (For capitalization rules, turn to 404.1-407.3 in *Write Source 2000*.)

1   Baseball legends like babe ruth, hank aaron, roger maris, mark

2   McGwire, and sammy sosa have helped make baseball an all-american

3   pastime. for years fans have crowded into stadiums around the country to

4   witness these home-run hitters at their best.

5   one of the most gifted and popular players of all time was babe ruth.

6   babe's real name was george herman ruth, and he was born in baltimore,

7   maryland. babe ruth pitched for the boston red sox, played outfield for the

8   new york yankees, and even coached for the brooklyn dodgers. though ruth

9   was very talented in all these areas, the thing he is most remembered for is

10   his home-run hitting. his record of 60 home runs in one season was

11   unchallenged until 1962 when roger maris, another american league player,

12   broke the record with 61 home runs in one season. babe ruth was elected to

13   the baseball hall of fame in 1936.

14   today, records continue to be broken by modern baseball legends such as

15   mark mcgwire and sammy sosa. these two players both broke maris's record

16   in september 1998. mcgwire, who was born in pomona, california, on october

17   1, 1963, plays first base for the st. louis cardinals. he ended his 1998 season

18   with a new record of 70 home runs, while sosa finished the season with 66

19   home runs. mcgwire said in an interview with the st. louis dispatch,

20 ^T"this is a season I will never, ever forget, and I hope everybody in baseball

21 never forgets." ^Bbaseball fans won't soon forget these talented players. ^Nnot

22 only are they power hitters, but they have also demonstrated to their fans

23 what it means to play with dignity, class, and humility.

24 ^Aalthough ^Mmc^Ggwire hit more home runs than ^Ssosa, ^Ssosa was voted the

25 1998 ^Nnational ^Lleague ^Mmost ^Vvaluable ^Pplayer by the ^Bbaseball ^Wwriters

26 ^Aassociation of ^Aamerica. ^Aat ^Wwrigley ^Ffield, ^Ssosa said, "^Wwinning the ~~mvp~~ ^{MVP} is not

27 for me; it's for the people of the city of ^Cchicago." ^Bbesides his 66 homers, ^Ssosa

28 led the major leagues with 158 ~~rbi's~~ ^{RBI's} and took the ^Ccubs to the ^Nnational

29 ^Lleague play-offs.

30 ^Ssosa is from ^Ssan ^Ppedro de ^Mmacoris in the ^Ddominican ^Rrepublic. ^Aafter the

31 1998 baseball season, ^Ssosa helped the victims of ^Hhurricane ^Ggeorge. ^Hhe

32 raised money to buy food for people in the ^Ddominican ^Rrepublic and other

33 ^Ccaribbean countries. ^Ssosa also asked the ^Jjapanese government to send

34 1,000 prefab houses to the ^Ddominican ^Rrepublic.

35 ^Ppeople in the ^Uunited ^Sstates also benefited from this historic home-run

36 derby. ^Sseven of ^Ssosa and ^Mmc^Ggwire's home-run balls were auctioned off. ^Tthe

37 money from ^Ssosa's home-run ball 61 went to the ^Ssammy ^Ssosa ^Ffoundation, an

38 organization that helps kids. ^Hhalf the money paid for ^Bbig ^Mmac's number 70

39 home-run ball also went to charity.

Plurals and Spelling

Developing spelling skills takes time and patience. Using your spell checker and a dictionary can help, but following the guidelines below will also improve your spelling skills. (Turn to 408.1-409.3 and 411.1-411.4 in *Write Source 2000* to review rules about spelling correctly. Also use the guide on pages 412-418.)

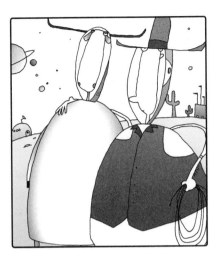

| **Directions** | In the following sentences, underline the correctly spelled word in parentheses. The first sentence has been done for you. |

1. At (<u>rodeos</u>, *rodeoes*), cowboys show their skills at (*handleing*, <u>handling</u>) cattle.

2. At these competitions, (*rideing*, <u>riding</u>) skills are important.

3. Steer (*wrestleing*, <u>wrestling</u>) is a popular event for competitors.

4. (<u>Bulldogging</u>, *Bulldoging*) is another name for this event.

5. In this event, the cowboy tries (<u>grabbing</u>, *grabing*) the horns of the steer to twist the head of the animal to one side.

6. This causes the steer to lose its balance, (<u>forcing</u>, *forceing*) the animal to fall to the ground.

7. Calf (*ropeing*, <u>roping</u>) is another important skill for ranchers and cowboys.

8. The cowboy (*lassoes*, <u>lassos</u>) the calf with a (<u>looped</u>, *loopped*) rope.

9. The cowboy then (<u>ties</u>, *tys*) together three of the calf's (<u>feet</u>, *feets*).

10. In barrel (<u>racing</u>, *raceing*), competitors ride horses in a pattern between and around barrels.

11. Some may (<u>believe</u>, *beleive*) that these competitions are dangerous for the animals.

All Write pp. 333-335 and 344

12. However, the people who practice these skills are (*careful, carful*) not to hurt the animals.

13. While (*battleing, battling*) these animals, the cowboys are practicing skills that will help them in (*raiseing, raising*) their livestock.

14. My family and (*freinds, friends*) are (*committed, commited*) to helping (*children, childrens*) understand the sport.

15. My (*sisters-in-law, sister-in-laws*) tell (*stories, storys*) of exciting rodeo events.

16. In junior rodeos, children rope goats instead of (*calves, calfs*), but (*niether, neither*) of those animals is easy to rope.

17. A rodeo clown can throw (*handfuls, handsful*) of confetti or (*tomatos, tomatoes*) to distract angry bulls.

18. At the (*beginning, begining*) of their act, some clowns play musical instruments such as (*banjoes, banjos*), harmonicas, or guitars.

19. Rodeo cowboys compete by riding (*steers, steeres*), bulls, and broncos.

20. Professional rodeo cowboys buy (*their, thier*) hats and boots at the many Cowboy Country Stores located in the western United States.

Next Step Write a paragraph about an interesting sports event. Share the paragraph with a classmate. Ask the classmate to check your writing for correct spelling and use of plurals.

Using the Right Word 1

When is it important to know if one word (such as *good*) should be used instead of another word (*well*)? The answer to that is easy. It's important to use the right word whenever you are going to share your thoughts in a formal or semiformal situation.

Whenever you have a usage question, refer to "Using the Right Word," 419.1-433.5 in *Write Source 2000*.

Directions   If the underlined word is incorrect, cross out the word and write the correct form above it.   Do not change a word that is correct. The first sentence has been done for you.

1. On a hot summer morning in 1939, the people who lived in tiny Orange
   City, Iowa, were ~~already~~ *all ready* for the ~~biannual~~ *annual* Fourth of July celebration.

2. In the village park, a large ~~blew~~ *blue* cannon lay on a frame between two
   wooden-spoked wheels.

3. ~~Besides~~ *Beside* the big gun, three huge balls rested on a square wooden ~~bass~~ *base*.

4. Two uniformed World War I veterans stood on either side of the cannon.   A
   large ~~amount~~ *number* of spectators had gathered around them to watch the

   traditional opening exercise.

5. The mayor, who also ran the Farmers Co-op Elevator, was just finishing his
   speech: " . . . and the reason we're ~~altogether~~ *all together* in this safe, free, grand

   country of ours is not simply a result of this being our place of birth."

6. "As ~~alot~~ *a lot* of you older folks remember, when President Wilson told us to take
   up arms, we all willingly ~~excepted~~ *accepted* that command."

All Write pp. 345-360

7. "We ~~new~~ *knew* that the enemy guns and tanks and subs would cause deaths."

8. "And we all had a fear of this ~~pane~~ *pain*, but more important, we <u>knew</u> that the

   <u>principle</u> of our freedom was at stake!"

9. "When the call to duty came, we believed that free people cannot remain

   free ~~buy~~ *by* simply watching others ~~brake~~ *break* up their democracy!"

10. The mayor unhooked his thumbs from the suspenders of his overalls and

    stabbed his large right hand into the air to emphasize his last point: "So our

    soldier boys ~~brought~~ *took* their guns and bullets over to the other side of the ocean,

    so they could ~~take~~ *bring* back a new lease on freedom to this side of the ocean!"

11. The crowd, composed of farmers in striped suspender pants, housewives in

    freshly ironed aprons, a <u>number</u> of storekeepers, and ~~alot~~ *a lot* of children, had

    never seemed ~~board~~ *bored* during the speech.

12. And now, ~~altogether~~ *all together*, they cheered the mayor ~~that~~ *who* gave the speech; and they

    cheered the round-shouldered veteran who lit the fuse; and they cheered the

    ~~blew~~ *blue* smoke that exploded out of the huge, old cannon.

13. But most of all, they cheered the notion that each one of them had just fired

    the gun ~~who~~ *that* silenced the enemy and brought ~~piece~~ *peace*.

Next Step Write a short observation report about a recent incident that delighted (or frustrated) you. Use five or more of the words you just learned about in this lesson. Circle them. (See pages 209-212 in *Write Source 2000* for writing guidelines and a sample observation report.)

Using the Right Word 2

Directions Correct any errors by drawing a line through the error and writing the correct form above it. Do not change any word that is correct. (For explanations and examples, turn to 419.1-433.5 in *Write Source 2000*.) The first sentence has been done for you.

1. Do members of your family often ~~set~~ *sit* down to ~~right~~ *write* letters?

2. Are you ~~sum one which~~ *someone who* enjoys communicating ~~threw~~ *through* the mail?

3. Does your heart beat faster when you catch ~~site~~ *sight* of a letter addressed to you?

4. When ~~your~~ *you're* in the act of taking a letter out of the mailbox, ~~wear~~ *where* do you look

   first: at the address, at the stamp, or at the return address?

5. Did you ever write ~~too~~ *to* a friend, ask for a prompt response, and ~~than waist~~ *then waste*

   the next three ~~weaks~~ *weeks* waiting for a reply?

6. Is ~~they're~~ *there* any way you can determine ~~weather~~ *whether* someone who writes about

   his or her success is attempting to impress you, or simply attempting to be

   friendly and ~~personnel~~ *personal*?

7. Some people enjoy writing letters so much that they'll ~~steel~~ *steal* time out of a

   busy day and write such a long letter that it exceeds the postal ~~wait~~ *weight* limits.

8. A letter that exceeds the ~~wait~~ *weight* limit will have ~~too~~ *to* have extra postage.

9. If a letter ~~seams~~ *seems* heavy, have the post office weigh it.

10. If that happens to you, try using lighter ~~stationary~~; *stationery* then mailing the letter

    won't cost so much.

All Write pp. 345-360

Using the Right Word 3

Directions If the underlined word is incorrect, cross out the word and write the correct form above it.   Do not change a word that is correct. (For examples and explanations, turn to 419.1-433.5 in *Write Source 2000*.)   The first sentence has been done for you.

1. We've all ~~herd~~ *heard* words of wisdom like "Work hard" and "Plan ahead."

2. The longer you ~~lay~~ *lie* in bed after the sun rises, the ~~less~~ *fewer* things you'll accomplish ~~buy~~ *by* day's end.

3. Don't rely on someone else to say, "~~Leave~~ *Let* me do that for you." Do for yourself; you'll be much ~~farther~~ *further* along.

4. If all of ~~you're~~ *your* eggs are in one basket, make sure you don't lose that basket.

5. I've ~~scene~~ *seen* it all—from the Great Depression when you couldn't ~~by~~ *buy* a job to the postwar boom when people looked past some jobs in favor of others.

6. Keep ~~you're~~ *your* own house in order, and you'll get along ~~good~~ *well* with others.

7. ~~Its~~ *It's* a good idea to respect the ~~rites~~ *rights* of your neighbors.   Treat them ~~like~~ *as* you want them to treat you.

8. At your age, I was not ~~aloud~~ *allowed* to date.   My brother was my ~~mail~~ *male* escort to all of the school dances.

9. When the ~~whether~~ *weather* turns cold, always ~~where~~ *wear* a hat and two ~~pears~~ *pairs* of socks.

10. ~~They're~~ *Their* friends are arranging a surprise party at Bill and Bertha's favorite restaurant, and ~~there~~ *they're* also arranging to take them ~~their~~ *there* in a limo.

Using the Right Word Review 1

Correct any errors by drawing a line through the error and writing the correct form above it. Do not change any word that is correct. (For examples and explanations, turn to 419.1-433.5 in *Write Source 2000*.) The first sentence has been done for you.

1. I was happy about the birth of my ~~deer~~ *dear* little brother, at least ~~four~~ *for* a while.

2. ~~Know~~ *No* one told me, of ~~coarse~~ *course*, that he ~~wood~~ *would* grow up ~~too~~ *to* be a little nuisance.

3. It was a big ~~pane~~ *pain* to take care of Leon.

4. "But ~~your~~ *you're* such a good baby-sitter," my mom would ~~council~~ *counsel* me.

5. "Now be sure to tell me if Leon starts ~~braking~~ *breaking* things or digging ~~wholes~~ *holes* in the neighbor's yard again . . . or starts eating those plants."

6. The neighbors were ~~all together~~ *altogether* [completely] amazed by my little brother.

7. One day Leon sat down as ~~piecefully~~ *peacefully* as could be ~~rite~~ *right* in the middle of Mr. Ganetzke's garden and ate one beet leaf after another. It was quite a ~~site~~ *sight*.

8. He may have stripped that garden ~~bear~~ *bare*, but I had a nose for catching him doing anything wrong, and I always told on him.

9. ~~Its plane too~~ *It's plain to* me that Leon would ~~chose~~ *choose* to eat bugs instead of ~~meet~~ *meat*.

10. Why did I have to be ~~choosen~~ *chosen* to be his bodyguard?

11. It ~~seamed~~ *seemed* to me that ~~accept~~ *except* for my birthday, Christmas, and the ~~Forth~~ *Fourth* of July, life wasn't very fair.

12. Yes, life with Leon is a continuous ~~pane~~ *pain*, but of ~~coarse~~ *course*, I am getting used to him.

13. Looking at the little rug rat ~~laying~~ *lying* there, I don't ~~no whose~~ *know who's* going to ~~loose~~ *lose* this battle.

All Write pp. 345-360

Using the Right Word Review 2

Correct any errors by drawing a line through the error and writing the correct form above it. Do not change any word that is correct. (For examples and explanations, turn to 419.1-433.5 in *Write Source 2000*.) The first sentence has been done for you.

1. Middle school presented me with a ~~vary~~ *very* real problem.

2. I didn't ~~no~~ *know* how ~~too~~ *to* do a pull-up; of ~~coarse~~ *course*, that wasn't the ~~hole~~ *whole* problem.

3. I was put off by tests of physical strength and fitness; but, ~~weather~~ *whether* I liked it ~~ore~~ *or* not, fitness tests were part of physical education, a required ~~coarse~~ *course*.

4. I was to be graded on something I showed ~~know~~ *no* talent ~~four~~ *for*.

5. I sure needed ~~sum~~ *some* good ~~council~~ *counsel* [advice] on living ~~threw~~ *through* fitness tests.

6. After several ~~vane~~ *vain* [worthless] attempts at convincing our family doctor to ~~right~~ *write* me two weeks' worth of excuses, I had to ~~except~~ *accept* the facts.

7. My ~~moral~~ *morale* [personal attitude] was low on the first ~~mourning~~ *morning* of the tests, but I began ~~two~~ *to* feel a little better about things later.

8. My teacher counseled [advised] me on the ~~rite~~ *right* way ~~too~~ *to* do a pull-up.

9. He even gave me a compliment when I ~~razed~~ *raised* my chin well above the bar.

10. I didn't do very ~~good~~ *well* on the other tests.

11. Running gives me ~~soar~~ *sore* ankles, so the mile run was ~~vary~~ *very* hard.

12. ~~Its~~ *It's* a good thing we had a fire drill before the final test—push-ups.

13. During the fire drill, I decided I would ~~immigrate~~ *emigrate* to a ~~hole~~ *whole* new country.

14. It did no good as I had to do the push-ups anyway; so it was ~~quiet~~ *quite* a ~~mourning~~ *morning*.

15. As the ~~principle~~ *principal* watched me prove my mettle, my bones ~~creeked~~ *creaked* and my arms went numb.

Sentence Activities

The activities in this section cover four important areas: (1) the basic parts, types, and kinds of sentences; (2) methods for writing smooth-reading sentences; (3) common sentence errors; and (4) ways to add variety to sentences. Most activities include a main practice part in which you review, combine, or analyze different sentences. In addition, the **Next Step** activities give you follow-up practice with certain skills.

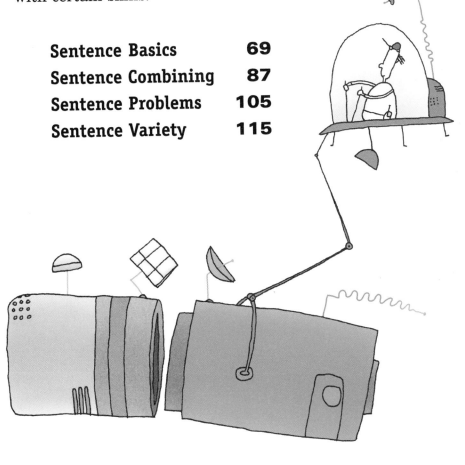

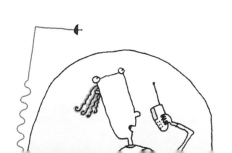

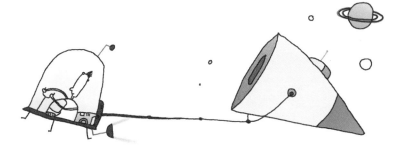

Subjects and Predicates 1

Good writers write clear and complete sentences. A sentence consists of two parts: the subject and the predicate. The **subject** is the part that is doing something or about which something is being said. The **predicate** is the part that says something about the subject. In a sentence, the subject and predicate fit together to form a complete thought. (Turn to 434.1-435.7 and 446.3 in *Write Source 2000* to examine subjects and predicates in more detail.)

EXAMPLES

Simple Subject:

<u>Marjorie</u> owns a robot that carries her books for her.

(The simple subject is who or what the sentence is about.)

Understood Subject:

Think about what a robot could do in your home. (understood subject: <u>You</u>)

(When the sentence is a command or a request, the subject is usually not stated. The person to whom the command is directed—*You*—is the subject of the sentence.)

Simple Predicate:

Felicia's robot <u>will obey</u> all her commands.

(The predicate—or verb—tells something about the subject. *Remember:* helping verbs like *will* are often part of the simple predicate.)

Directions In the following sentences, underline the simple subject once and the simple predicate twice. The first sentence has been done for you.

1. <u>Robots</u> <u>work</u> in homes, businesses, and schools.

2. In medical laboratories, <u>robots</u> <u>handle</u> hazardous materials.

3. At the General Motors Corporation, <u>robots</u> <u>work</u> on assembly lines performing tasks like welding and painting.

All Write pp. 368-369 and 383

4. Most boring or dangerous <u>tasks</u> <u>are done</u> by GMC's robots.

5. Other <u>companies</u> <u>use</u> specially designed robots for tasks that require precision.

6. <u>Robots</u> <u>explore</u> sunken ships, distant planets, and active volcanoes.

7. Miguel's toy <u>soldier</u> <u>is</u> really a small robot.

8. <u>Think</u> of all the toys you own that are really tiny robots. (You)

9. <u>Jeremiah</u> <u>dreams</u> of owning his own robot someday.

10. <u>Elena</u> <u>wishes</u> for a robot to do her math homework for her.

11. <u>I</u> <u>want</u> a robot that will mow my lawn, deliver my newspapers, and clean my room.

12. Maybe my <u>teacher</u> <u>will be replaced</u> by a computerized robot.

13. <u>Imagine</u> what the world would be like if we all owned robots. (You)

14. <u>One</u> of the stars of *The Red Planet* <u>was</u> Robby the Robot.

15. <u>Have</u> <u>you</u> ever <u>seen</u> a robot at work?

16. When I get home, our family's <u>robot</u> <u>gets</u> me a glass of milk.

17. Most <u>robots</u> in films and TV shows <u>are</u> not very realistic.

18. <u>Can</u> <u>you</u> <u>name</u> your favorite robot?

Next Step Imagine having your own robot. Write a paragraph describing what your personal robot would be like. Then draw an illustration to accompany your paragraph. Share the illustration and the paragraph with a classmate. Have your classmate check your writing for complete sentences.

Subjects and Predicates 2

There are simple subjects and simple predicates. But what about all those other words in the sentence? The words that describe the subject or predicate are called *modifiers*. Modifiers change or add to the meaning of the subject or predicate. Together, the simple subject plus its modifiers make the **complete subject,** and the simple predicate plus its modifiers make the **complete predicate.** (Turn to 435.1 and 435.5 in *Write Source 2000* for more information.)

EXAMPLES

Complete Subject:
The large, umbrella-shaped parachute saved the life of the inexperienced pilot.

(The complete subject is the simple subject—*parachute*—plus all its modifiers.)

Complete Predicate:
The large, umbrella-shaped parachute *saved the life of the inexperienced pilot.*

(The complete predicate is the simple predicate—*saved*—plus all its modifiers.)

Directions	In the following sentences, underline the simple subject once and the simple predicate twice. Then divide the complete subject and the complete predicate with a slash (/). The first sentence has been done for you.

1. French aeronaut Jean Pierre Blanchard /dropped a dog in the first parachute "jump" in 1785.

2. Blanchard /successfully made the first human parachute drop in 1793.

3. Parachutes /are now required for all balloonists and pilots.

4. The large silk or nylon parachute canopy /has a small vent hole in its center that expands when the parachute opens to lessen the shock of the rapid fall.

All Write p. 369

5. The 24-foot, multipaneled parachute/is pulled from the jumper's backpack by a smaller parachute.

6. Parachutes/have been used during wars to drop troops, tanks, and equipment behind enemy lines.

7. Sport parachuting, also known as skydiving,/became popular in the 1970s.

8. Steerable parachutes that allow safer landings/have made the sport even more popular today.

9. Parachutists/compete in skydiving competitions by doing a series of aerobatic maneuvers before reaching parachute-opening altitude.

10. Teams of free-falling skydivers/compete by forming as many geometric patterns as possible before opening their chutes.

11. (You)/Consider the risk of skydiving before taking the plunge.

12. Steerable parachutes/are quite different from hang gliders.

13. In 1972, a Yugoslavian flight attendant/survived a fall from 33,370 feet without a parachute.

14. The record for the longest fall with a parachute/is 40 minutes.

Next Step Skydiving is a sport that requires skill and daring. Write a paragraph explaining why you would or would not want to be a skydiver. Share the paragraph with a classmate. Be sure to write in complete sentences.

Compound Subjects and Predicates

Combining short, related sentences into longer sentences is valuable practice for improving your writing style. Writers can combine short sentences using coordinating conjunctions. This can result in a sentence with either a **compound subject** (two or more simple subjects) or a **compound predicate** (two or more simple predicates) or both. (For more information about compound subjects and compound predicates, see 435.2 and 435.6-435.7 in *Write Source 2000*.)

EXAMPLES

Compound Subject:
Earl and Kultida Woods are the proud parents of golf champion Tiger Woods.

Compound Predicate:
Tiger Woods putted against Bob Hope at age two and was featured in *Golf Digest* at age five.

Compound Subject and Compound Predicate:
Tiger and his father play golf and support charities.

Directions   In the following sentences, underline the subject with one line and the predicate with two lines. Remember that some sentences have only a compound subject, some have only a compound predicate, and some have both. The first one has been done for you.

1. Tiger Woods became a professional golfer and won two PGA Tour victories in 1996.

2. Keenan and Angelica watched Tiger play in the tournament and got his autograph at the ninth hole.

3. Last year Tiger and his family traveled to the Asian Honda Classic Golf Tournament in Thailand.

All Write p. 369

4. In just one year, <u>Tiger</u> <u>won</u> several tournaments, <u>made</u> a lot of money, and <u>earned</u> the respect of other professional golfers.

5. Tiger's <u>father</u> and <u>mother</u> <u>taught</u> him that all people deserve the chance to live out their dreams.

6. <u>Tiger</u> and his <u>father</u> <u>created</u> and actively <u>support</u> a foundation that gives minorities opportunities to play golf.

7. Many <u>awards</u>, <u>trophies</u>, and <u>medals</u> <u>decorate</u> Tiger's home.

8. In their spare time, <u>Tiger</u> and his <u>friends</u> <u>play</u> basketball and <u>go</u> fishing.

9. <u>Mary Lou Retton</u>, the gymnast, and <u>Tiger Woods</u> <u>are</u> the two youngest athletes to be named "Sportsperson of the Year" by *Sports Illustrated*.

10. Young <u>men</u> and <u>women</u> <u>admire</u> Tiger for both his skill and his modesty.

11. <u>Can</u> <u>you</u> or your <u>friend</u> <u>think</u> of a more exciting golfer than Tiger?

12. Over the past few years, <u>Tiger</u> <u>has played</u> well and <u>created</u> a renewed interest in golf.

13. Young <u>people</u> and old <u>people</u> alike <u>admire</u> Tiger's talent and <u>enjoy</u> watching him play.

14. Because of his popularity, many <u>companies</u> and nonprofit <u>organizations</u> <u>have asked</u> Tiger to be a spokesperson for them.

Next Step Using the Internet or other sources, research a sports or entertainment figure. Write a paragraph or two about your findings using some compound subjects and compound predicates. Share your writing with a classmate and ask him or her to check for complete sentences and proper use of compound subjects and predicates.

Phrases

A phrase is a group of words that lacks a subject, a predicate, or both. In most cases, a phrase works as a modifier in a sentence. The most common type of phrase is the prepositional phrase. Every prepositional phrase begins with a preposition (*in, at, by, with,* etc.) and ends with the object of the preposition (the nearest noun or pronoun). In between may be words that modify the object of the preposition. Study the examples below and the ones in your handbook for more information. (Turn to 437.1-437.2 and 455.1-455.3 in *Write Source 2000.*)

. . . and a large order of phrases

EXAMPLES

Our trip to North Dakota was great.
(preposition: *to*; object: *North Dakota*; phrase modifies: *trip*)

We stopped at many drive-in restaurants.
(preposition: *at*; object: *restaurants;* phrase modifies: *stopped*)

Directions Underline the prepositional phrases in the sentences that follow. Circle each preposition. Draw an arrow to each object of a preposition. (The number of prepositional phrases is listed in parentheses after each sentence.) The first sentence has been done for you.

1. Early (in) the morning, the Phillips family left (for) the airport. (2)

2. They waited (at) the busy airport to catch their flight (to) Disney World. (2)

3. (During) their wait, they talked (about) the special attractions (at) Epcot. (3)

4. Mikah desperately wanted to see all (of) the World Showcase, which

   features the cultures (of) 11 different countries. (2)

5. Epcot is an exciting and educational experience (for) everyone

   (of) every age. (2)

All Write pp. 371 and 398

6. Operating (on) a tight budget, Mikah and Ruby's parents are determined

not to spend too much money (on) this vacation. (2)

7. (With) a tour package, they were able to save money (on) entrance passes

(to) Disney World. (3)

8. Ruby has been dreaming (about) this magical vacation (for) years. (2)

9. The Phillips will be vacationing (in) Disney World (for) five days. (2)

| **Directions** | Write 4 sentences below about a trip you took (or would like to take). Underline the prepositional phrases, circle the prepositions, and draw an arrow to each object of a preposition. |

1. _____

_____

_____

2. _____

_____

_____

3. _____

_____

_____

4. _____

_____

_____

Clauses

Clauses, like phrases, are word groups that add information to a sentence. Unlike phrases, clauses always have a subject and a predicate. Clauses that form a complete thought are called **independent clauses,** and clauses that do not form a complete thought are called **dependent** or **subordinate clauses.** (*Write Source 2000* gives more information about clauses in 436.3 and 437.3 - 438.2.)

EXAMPLES

Dependent Clause:

Even though she was at the peak of her career, Florence Griffith-Joyner retired from running in 1989.

Independent Clause:

Florence Griffith-Joyner retired from running in 1989 even though she was at the peak of her career.

Florence Griffith-Joyner was a fantastic runner, and she won many Olympic medals.
(Two independent clauses are separated by a comma and a coordinating conjunction or by a semicolon.)

| **Directions** | In each of the following sentences, identify the italicized clause. Write *I* for independent or *D* for dependent. The first sentence has been done for you. |

_____I_____ **1.** Though she grew up in a poor section of South Los Angeles, *Joyner overcame poverty to become a world-class runner.*

_____I_____ **2.** *Florence Joyner was known by the nickname "FloJo,"* but sports fans also knew her as the fastest woman in the world.

_____D_____ **3.** *After she won the silver medal in the 200-meter dash in the 1984 Olympics,* Joyner retired from her running career.

All Write pp. 370 and 372

_____I_____ **4.** She began competing again in 1987, and *she earned second place at the World Championship Games in Rome.*

_____I_____ **5.** *Joyner competed in the 1988 Olympics in Seoul,* and she won gold medals in the 100- and 200-meter races and in the 400-meter relay.

_____D_____ **6.** What do you think of the outfits Florence wore *when she ran?*

_____I_____ **7.** After she retired from running, *Florence became interested in writing and modeling.*

_____D_____ **8.** *Although she officially retired from competition in 1989,* Florence continued to coach her husband, Al Joyner, who is a world-champion jumper.

_____D_____ **9.** *While she slept,* Florence Griffith-Joyner died of a heart seizure on September 21, 1998.

_____I_____ **10.** *Florence Griffith-Joyner will always be remembered as a running legend,* and she will be admired as a person who always gave her best effort.

Next Step Do some research using the Internet or another source to discover more about Joyner. Try to write five sentences using dependent and independent clauses. Share your writing with a classmate and check each other's work for correct use of clauses.

Misplaced Modifiers

Modifiers are words, phrases, and clauses that describe the simple subject or simple predicate of the sentence. The key to using modifiers effectively is to make sure that you place them as close as possible to the words they modify. Misplacing the modifier makes the sentence confusing and sometimes silly. (Turn to page 91 in *Write Source 2000* to examine misplaced modifiers in more detail.)

HAPPY B

EXAMPLE

Confusing Sentence:
John Glenn returned to space shortly after turning 77 on October 29, 1998.
(It sounds as if John Glenn turned 77 on October 29, 1998.)

Clear Sentence:
Shortly after turning 77, John Glenn returned to space on October 29, 1998.

Directions   Rewrite the following sentences to correct the misplaced modifiers. The first one has been done for you.

1. John Glenn relaxed on the day before the flight with his family.

   On the day before the flight, John Glenn relaxed with his family.

2. He was eager to begin his second flight into space with all the media in attendance.

   With all the media in attendance, he was eager to begin his second

   flight into space.

3. After being away from flight for many years, the new space program was an opportunity that Glenn couldn't resist.

   After being away from flight for many years, Glenn couldn't resist an

   opportunity like the new space program.

   All Write pp. 54 and 370

4. The space crew spent the morning adjusting their bulky space suits along with John Glenn.

   The space crew, along with John Glenn, spent the morning adjusting

   their bulky space suits.

5. Because he's the oldest American astronaut to fly in space, one reporter is planning to publish a book about John Glenn and his flight.

   Because John Glenn is the oldest American astronaut to fly in space,

   one reporter is planning to publish a book about him and his flight.

6. Many local residents were able to watch the launch of the space shuttle from their own backyards.

   From their own backyards, many local residents were able to watch

   the launch of the space shuttle.

7. Wearing bulky space suits, the ground crew helped the astronauts board the shuttle.

   Wearing bulky space suits, the astronauts boarded the shuttle with

   the help of the ground crew.

8. The president of the United States came to watch the space shuttle lift off with a congressional delegation.

   The president of the United States, with a congressional delegation,

   came to watch the space shuttle lift off.

Next Step John Glenn was the first U.S. astronaut to orbit the earth. Using the Internet or other research tools, find out more about him and his career. Then write a paragraph about your findings. Ask a classmate to check your writing for misplaced modifiers.

Types of Sentences 1

Good writers vary the lengths of their sentences. Using too many short sentences makes writing choppy; however, using too many long sentences can make writing confusing. When you write, try to mix **simple, compound, complex,** and **compound-complex** sentences to achieve variety and clarity. (Turn to 437.3 - 438.2 in *Write Source 2000* for more on types of sentences.)

EXAMPLES

Simple Sentence:
Jack and Maria love in-line skating.

Compound Sentence:
They play on a roller-hockey team, and they enjoy the competition.

Complex Sentence:
Although they are amateurs now, Jack and Maria dream of being professional skaters someday.

Compound-Complex Sentence:
Because they are determined to fulfill their dream, Jack and Maria practice daily, and they read everything that they can find about skating.

Note: A compound-complex sentence contains two or more independent clauses and one or more dependent clauses.

Directions Label the following sentences with *S* for simple, *C* for compound, *CX* for complex, and *CC* for compound-complex. The first sentence has been done for you.

S **1.** Joseph Merlin, a Dutchman, invented roller skates in the eighteenth century.

CX **2.** After he studied the design of ice skates, Joseph fastened wooden spools in the place of the ice-skate blades.

All Write p. 372

_CC_   **3.** In 1763, metal wheels replaced the wooden spools, and in 1863, American inventor James Leonard Plimpton created rocking skates that allowed the skater to maneuver more easily.

_C_   **4.** Ball-bearing wheels were introduced late in the nineteenth century, and, as a result, roller-skating became even more popular.

_S_   **5.** Skateboards and in-line skates are modifications of roller skates.

_S_   **6.** Skateboards are short, wide boards made of wood, plastic, or fiberglass.

_C_   **7.** In-line skates were first manufactured in the 1980s, and they have become very popular with people of all ages.

_CX_   **8.** Although roller-skating has not been accepted as an Olympic sport, athletes can compete in events like short-track speed skating with other roller skaters.

_CX_   **9.** Roller Derby, which is also popular among skaters, is a competition between two teams of five men and five women on roller skates.

_CC_   **10.** Because Roller Derby was so popular in the 1950s, fans flocked to indoor rinks to watch, or they stayed home and watched on their televisions.

Next Step Find out more about Roller Derby, speed skating, or roller hockey by using the Internet or other sources. Write a paragraph about your findings and share your writing with a classmate. Ask your classmate to label the types of sentences you used in your paragraph.

Types of Sentences 2

Sentence combining is one of the most valuable skills you can develop as a writer. With practice, you can combine short, choppy sentences into longer, smoother-reading sentences. One of the most efficient kinds of sentences to form when combining is the **complex sentence.** Complex sentences contain one independent clause and one or more dependent clauses. (Turn to page 96 and 438.1 in your *Write Source 2000* for more information.)

Directions   Combine the following short sentences by adding the subordinate conjunction indicated in the parentheses. The first one has been done for you.

1. Visitors have been coming to Vancouver Island for years. Few know about the excellent surfing locations. (**Although**)

   Although visitors have been coming to Vancouver Island for years,

   few know about the excellent surfing locations.

2. The sun rose. Frank began to hike the trails. (**as soon as**)

   As soon as the sun rose, Frank began to hike the trails.

3. He planned to go hunting. He changed his plans so he could take his daughter skiing. (**although**)

   Although he planned to go hunting, he changed his plans so he could

   take his daughter skiing.

4. There are many outdoor activities. People keep very busy and very fit on Vancouver Island. (**because**)

   Because there are many outdoor activities, people keep very busy and

   very fit on Vancouver Island.

     All Write pp. 58 and 372

5. It rains a lot on the coast. The hillsides are always green. (**because**)

Because it rains a lot on the coast, the hillsides are always

green.

6. The weather is unpredictable. Residents of Vancouver Island are always prepared for rain or sunshine. (**because**)

Because the weather is unpredictable, residents of Vancouver Island

are always prepared for rain or sunshine.

7. Kayakers skim across the rivers. Skiers swish down the slopes. (**while**)

While kayakers skim across the rivers, skiers swish down the

slopes.

8. Vancouver Island is located on the Pacific coast. It is an excellent place to view killer whales. (**because**)

Because Vancouver Island is located on the Pacific coast, it is an

excellent place to view killer whales.

9. The tourists enjoyed a morning of whale watching. They visited the Parliament Building and had tea at the Empress Hotel. (**after**)

After the tourists enjoyed a morning of whale watching, they visited

the Parliament Building and had tea at the Empress Hotel.

Next Step Write a paragraph about your favorite vacation spot. Use short, simple sentences in your paragraph. Then exchange your paragraph with a classmate. Ask your classmate to revise your paragraph by combining the short sentences into complex sentences.

Kinds of Sentences

Sentences can be distinguished by their purpose. Some sentences ask questions (**interrogative**), some are statements (**declarative**), some give commands (**imperative**), and some are exclamations (**exclamatory**). As a writer, you choose the kind of sentence you want based on the message you want to give to the reader. (Turn to 438.3 - 438.6 in *Write Source 2000* to examine the four kinds of sentences in more detail.)

EXAMPLES

Declarative Sentence:
Tornadoes are among the most destructive natural disasters.

Imperative Sentence:
Head for shelter immediately when a tornado warning is issued.

Interrogative Sentence:
Do you know where the safest place in your home is during a tornado?

Exclamatory Sentence:
The tornado caused millions of dollars of damage in just three minutes!

Directions   Label the following sentences as *declarative, imperative, interrogative,* or *exclamatory*. Then add the correct end punctuation.   The first one has been done for you.

declarative   **1.** Tornadoes occur most often in the Plains States during the

spring and summer.

exclamatory   **2.** Tornado wind speeds can reach over 300 miles per hour!

imperative   **3.** To protect yourself, learn all you can about tornadoes.

declarative   **4.** The most violent tornadoes have more than one vortex or

rotating center.

interrogative   **5.** Did you know that in Mississippi three 40-passenger buses

were tossed over an eight-foot embankment during a tornado?

All Write p. 373

interrogative   **6.** Was anyone injured in the accident?

exclamatory   **7.** No, incredibly, no one was injured!

imperative   **8.** Stay away from windows and open spaces during a tornado.

interrogative   **9.** Have you heard of "Tornado Alley"?

declarative   **10.** This is an area between Nebraska and central Texas where tornadoes are most likely to occur.

declarative   **11.** Most tornadoes happen during the month of May, but the most deadly ones occur in April.

imperative   **12.** If you find yourself in an open field during a tornado, find a low spot immediately.

exclamatory   **13.** A tornado can drive a piece of straw through a wooden post!

declarative   **14.** Tornadoes are most common in the United States, the former Soviet Union, and Australia.

interrogative   **15.** If you are driving your car and the radio warns of a tornado in the area, what should you do?

exclamatory   **16.** Auntie Em, Auntie Em, it's a twister!

Next Step Tornadoes, hurricanes, and earthquakes are frightening natural disasters. With a classmate, devise a safety plan for your home to deal with the natural disaster most likely to occur in your area of the country. Share that plan with your family. Be sure to check your writing for complete sentences.

Sentence Combining with Key Words

Sometimes a single word can make a world of difference in a sentence. One added key word can provide just the extra touch needed to add impact to your sentence. If you have used two sentences to explain something, it's always a good idea to see if you can combine the two sentences by "borrowing" a key word from one and adding it to the other. Combining sentences by using key words can help you create more concise, mature sentences. (Turn to page 94 in *Write Source 2000*.)

EXAMPLES

Combining with an Adjective:
John's brother nibbles "munchies" between meals. He is <u>younger</u> than John.
John's *younger* brother nibbles "munchies" between meals.

Combining with a Participle:
Ji's dog scares people. Ji's dog <u>snarls</u>.
Ji's *snarling* dog scares people.
(*Snarls* has been changed to its participle form.)

Combining with an Adverb:
I passed my English test. I passed it <u>yesterday</u>.
***Yesterday,* I passed my English test.**

Directions   In each pair of sentences, underline the key word(s) in the second sentence and then move the form of that word (indicated in parentheses) to the first sentence.

1. Eligia did the exercises with ease. The exercises were <u>difficult</u>. *(adjective)*

   Eligia did the difficult exercises with ease.

2. I have to mow my overgrown lawn. I will mow the lawn <u>later</u>. *(adverb)*

   I have to mow my overgrown lawn later.

3. The fans stormed onto the field. The fans <u>screamed</u>. *(participle)*

   The screaming fans stormed onto the field.

4. Juan wrote an essay on endangered species. It <u>amazed</u> everyone. *(participle)*

Juan wrote an amazing essay on endangered species.

5. Jeison loves salsa. He loves it <u>hot</u> and <u>spicy</u>. *(adjective)*

Jeison loves hot and spicy salsa.

6. The crowd loved the play. The crowd <u>cheered</u>. *(participle)*

The cheering crowd loved the play.

7. I lost my wallet at the movies. I lost it <u>last week</u>. *(adverb)*

I lost my wallet at the movies last week.

8. The sun made me squint. The sun was <u>setting</u>. *(participle)*

The setting sun made me squint.

9. I changed the flat tire on the side of the road. I changed it <u>quickly</u>. *(adverb)*

I quickly changed the flat tire on the side of the road.

10. Bill's basket saved the game for us. He made it at the <u>last minute</u>. *(compound adjective)*

Bill's last-minute basket saved the game for us.

Next Step Write five pairs of sentences suitable for key word combining. Exchange your sentences with a classmate. Each of you should combine the sentences you received from your classmate.

Sentence Combining with a Series of Words or Phrases

Being able to combine shorter sentences into longer, more mature sentences is a great writing skill to learn. Longer sentences can help you show relationships that are hard to express in shorter sentences. To effectively combine short sentences, you need to recognize what the shorter sentences have in common—what series of words, phrases, or ideas can be pulled together into one longer sentence. Study the examples below. (Also turn to page 94 in *Write Source 2000* for more examples.)

EXAMPLES

Shorter Sentences:
Aaron skies on snow.
He skies on water.
He skies on ice.

Combined Sentence Using a Series of Words:
Aaron skies on snow, water, and ice.

Shorter Sentences:
Aaron sprained his ankle.
He bruised his hip.
He wrenched his back.

Combined Sentence Using a Series of Phrases:
Aaron sprained his ankle, bruised his hip, and wrenched his back.

Directions Combine the following sets of short sentences into longer ones using the method asked for in parentheses. The first one has been done for you.

1. John tore down the hill. He cut in front of Aaron. He caused him to fall.
   (Use a series of phrases.)

   John tore down the hill, cut in front of Aaron, and caused him to fall.

All Write p. 56

2. As Aaron tried to get out of John's way, he tumbled. Then he slid and spun. **(Use a series of words.)**

As Aaron tried to get out of John's way, he tumbled, slid, and spun.

3. John was skiing too fast. He was moving carelessly from side to side. He was taking unnecessary chances. **(Use a series of phrases.)**

John was skiing too fast, moving carelessly from side to side, and

taking unnecessary chances.

4. As John skied past Aaron, he whistled. He shouted and laughed. **(Use a series of words.)**

As John skied past Aaron, he whistled, shouted, and laughed.

5. The ski patrol headed up the hill with their toboggan. They brought a back brace. They also brought an inflatable leg cast. **(Use a series of phrases.)**

The ski patrol headed up the hill with their toboggan, a back brace,

and an inflatable leg cast.

6. Aaron now sits by himself. He watches hockey on television and dreams of getting back on the slopes. **(Use a series of phrases.)**

Aaron now sits by himself, watches hockey on televison, and dreams

of getting back on the slopes.

Next Step Write a paragraph describing an accident (or near accident) you have had. Then rewrite the paragraph to see how many sentences you can combine using a series of words or phrases as you did above. Compare your two paragraphs. Which one reads better?

Sentence Combining with Phrases

Experienced writers often combine short, simple sentences into longer, more meaningful ones by using a phrase in one of the sentences. The following types of phrases are often the key when it comes to sentence combining: **prepositional, participial, infinitive, and appositive phrases.** (Turn to page 95 and sections 451.2-451.3 and 455.1 in *Write Source 2000* to read about these phrases as you work on the sentences that follow.)

EXAMPLES

Infinitive Phrase:
I watched *to see it land*.
(*To see it land* is an infinitive phrase.)

Prepositional Phrase:
I watched *from my bedroom window*.
(*From my bedroom window* is a prepositional phrase.)

Appositive Phrase:
I watched from my bedroom window, *a great viewing place*.
(*A great viewing place* is an appositive phrase renaming "window.")

Participial Phrase:
***Wondering about the bird*, I watched from my bedroom window.**
(*Wondering about the bird* is a participial phrase describing "I.")

Combined Sentence:
Wondering about the bird, I watched from my bedroom window, a great viewing place, to see it land.

Directions   Combine each pair of simple sentences using the type of phrase indicated in the parentheses. The first sentence has been done for you.

1. The movie is scary. It is showing at the Hargrove Theater.
(participial phrase)

The movie showing at the Hargrove Theater is scary.

All Write pp. 57, 391, and 398

2. Frank and Phil waited for their pizza.   They are the famous Fettucini brothers. **(appositive phrase)**

Frank and Phil, the famous Fettucini brothers, waited for their pizza.

3. Glenna tore into a jelly-filled doughnut.   It was from the "chewy and gooey" shelf in the bakery. **(prepositional phrase)**

Glenna tore into a jelly-filled doughnut from the "chewy and gooey"

shelf in the bakery.

4. Terrance studied each mountain bike.   He wanted to determine which one would best meet his needs. **(infinitive phrase)**

Terrance studied each mountain bike to determine which one would

best meet his needs.

5. Alex blew a hole in one of his basketball shoes.   He was running down the court. **(participial phrase)**

Running down the court, Alex blew a hole in one of his basketball

shoes.

6. Josie's hair can be uncontrollable.   It is uncontrollable especially in wet weather. **(especially + a prepositional phrase)**

Josie's hair can be uncontrollable, especially in wet weather.

7. The Girls Next Door played at the last school dance.   They are music's answer to apple pie and sugar cookies. **(appositive phrase)**

The Girls Next Door, music's answer to apple pie and sugar cookies,

played at the last school dance.

Sentence Combining with Compound Subjects and Verbs

Sentences are not limited to having a single subject and predicate (or verb). A sentence can have two or more subjects called a **compound subject.** A sentence can also have a **compound verb.** Some sentences may have both a compound subject and a compound verb. Sometimes, instead of writing two short sentences, you may want to combine the subjects or verbs (or both) into a single sentence providing the same information.

Note: Notice how using a compound verb to combine the two sentences below eliminates repetition and lets you use one sentence instead of two.

EXAMPLE

Shorter Sentences:
I got up at 6:00 in the morning.
I got dressed in my warmest clothes.

Combined Sentence Using a Compound Verb:
I got up at 6:00 in the morning and dressed in my warmest clothes.

Directions   Combine each of the following pairs of sentences into a single sentence that uses compound subjects or verbs. Turn to pages 88 and 95 and to 435.2, 435.6, and 435.7 in *Write Source 2000* for more information and additional examples. Some sentences may require both a compound subject and compound verb. The first sentence has been done for you.

1. My dad was taking me ice fishing. My uncle was coming, too.

   My dad and my uncle were taking me ice fishing.

2. My dad made me a huge pancake-and-sausage breakfast. He asked if I was full.

   My dad made me a huge pancake-and-sausage breakfast and asked

   if I was full.

All Write pp. 48, 51, and 369

3. On the way to the lake, the two men told funny fishing stories. They poked fun at each other's fish tales.

On the way to the lake, the two men told funny fishing stories and

poked fun at each other's fish tales.

4. I believed only about half the stories. I laughed at all of them anyway.

I believed only about half the stories but laughed at all of them

anyway.

5. The heat in the car made me drowsy. The car's heat finally put me to sleep.

The heat in the car made me drowsy and finally put me to sleep.

6. At the lake, the cold wind cut right through my warm clothes. It caused my teeth to start chattering.

At the lake, the cold wind cut right through my warm clothes

and caused my teeth to start chattering.

7. My dad gathered kindling. My uncle helped and soon started a hot blazing fire.

My dad and uncle gathered kindling and soon started a hot blazing

fire.

8. I liked fishing that day. I enjoyed the warm fire even more.

I liked fishing that day but enjoyed the warm fire even more.

Next Step Write a paragraph describing an experience you have had in nature. Then rewrite the paragraph, combining sentences using compound subjects and verbs. Compare your two paragraphs and discuss the results with a classmate. Do each of you see an improvement in your rewritten versions?

Sentence Combining with Adjective Clauses

Using adjective clauses to combine simple sentences will help you avoid unnecessary repetition in your writing. (Adjective clauses begin with words like *who, whose, which,* and *that.*) But be careful. Too many *who*'s or *which*'s will make your writing sound textbookish.

Who, whose, which, and **that** are called *relative pronouns.* Look at section 444.1 in your *Write Source 2000* handbook for a definition of relative pronouns and then write that definition in the space provided below. (See page 96 and sections 444.1-445.2 for additional information.)

Definition: *A relative pronoun is both a . . . pronoun and a connecting*

word. It connects a subordinate clause to the main clause.

EXAMPLE

Shorter Sentences:
The ancient oak was destroyed in the storm.   It stood near the park entrance.

Combined Sentence Using an Adjective Clause:
The ancient oak *that stood at the park entrance* was destroyed in the storm.

(*That stood at the park entrance* is an adjective clause that modifies *oak.*)

Directions   Combine each pair of simple sentences into one complex sentence using *who, which,* or *that* as a connector.

1. The bearded wrestler gave his opponent a bear hug.   The bearded wrestler was slick with sweat.

    The bearded wrestler, who was slick with sweat, gave his opponent a

    bear hug.

2. The night air revived him after his day in the fields.   The air was cool and sweet smelling.

    The night air, which was cool and sweet smelling, revived him after his

    day in the fields.

All Write pp. 58, 360, and 382

3. The construction workers were treated for heat exhaustion. They were building the new road through the park.

   The construction workers who were building the new road through the

   park were treated for heat exhaustion.

4. The sun is the center of our solar system. The sun is 93 million miles away.

   The sun, which is 93 million miles away, is the center of our solar

   system.

5. The tracks led to the old miner's shack. The tracks were freshly made.

   The tracks, which were freshly made, led to the old miner's shack.

6. By the side of the road lay the ruined glider. It had been destined for Paris.

   By the side of the road lay the ruined glider that had been destined

   for Paris.

7. The agents escaped across the border. The agents set Mr. Goodwin free.

   The agents who set Mr. Goodwin free escaped across the border.

8. Rudy seldom checks out books. He would rather rap than read.

   Rudy, who would rather rap than read, seldom checks out books.

Next Step Many of the complex sentences you have made require commas. (The commas set off the adjective clause from the rest of the sentence.) Read about **restrictive** and **nonrestrictive clauses** in section 392.2 of your *Write Source 2000* handbook and check your sentences.

Sentence Combining with Adverb Clauses

Adverb clauses are used to form complex sentences. They answer *how, when, where, why, how much,* or *under what condition.* Adverb clauses can be used at the beginning or at the end of complex sentences. Subordinate conjunctions—words like *after, although, before*—are used to introduce adverb clauses. (For more information, turn to page 96 and to 456.3-456.4 in *Write Source 2000.*)

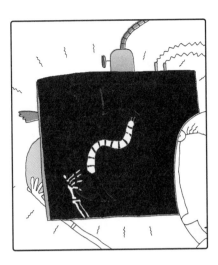

EXAMPLES

Shorter Sentences:
John checked the apple for wormholes. He ate the apple.

Combined Sentences:
***Before he ate the apple,* John checked it for wormholes.**
(An adverb clause at the beginning of a sentence needs a comma.)

John checked the apple for wormholes *before he ate the apple.*
(An adverb clause at the end of a sentence does not need a comma.)

Directions   Combine each of the following sets of short sentences into one sentence using the subordinate conjunction listed in the parentheses. The first one has been done for you.

Answers may vary.

1. I was about six years old. Something unforgettable happened. **(when)**

   When I was about six years old, something unforgettable happened.

2. Dad banged on my door. He yelled, "Get dressed and get downstairs!" **(as)**

   As Dad banged on my door, he yelled, "Get dressed and get downstairs!"

3. I realized I had forgotten my glasses. I was halfway down the stairs. **(before)**

   I was halfway down the stairs before I realized I had forgotten my glasses.

All Write pp. 58, 372, and 399

4. "What's wrong?" I asked.   I struggled to pull on my shoes. **(while)**

"What's wrong?" I asked while I struggled to pull on my shoes.

5. My dad turned and yelled, "Fire!"   He rushed out the front door. **(as)**

My dad turned and yelled, "Fire!" as he rushed out the front door.

6. He caught his breath.   He said, "The neighbor's house is on fire!" **(when)**

When he caught his breath, he said, "The neighbor's house is on fire!"

7. My heart was beating wildly in my throat.   I was still half asleep. **(although)**

Although I was still half asleep, my heart was beating wildly in my

throat.

8. I was hit by a blast of hot, smoky wind.   I followed my dad outside. **(as)**

I was hit by a blast of hot, smoky wind as I followed my dad outside.

9. I was awake by then.   I still hoped this was all a dream. **(although)**

Although I was awake by then, I still hoped this was all a dream.

Next Step   Write a paragraph about fire.   Maybe you have been involved in a fire.   Maybe you have a relative who is a firefighter.   Exchange your writing with a classmate.   On your classmate's paper, look for ideas that might be combined using adverb clauses.   Checkmark those ideas. When you get your paper back, try to combine the checkmarked ideas.

Combining Sentences into Complex Sentences

Complex sentences are made up of an independent and a dependent clause. The independent clause in a complex sentence contains the most important idea in the sentence. The dependent clause contains a less important idea. The two clauses can be combined with a relative pronoun such as *who, whose, which,* or *that.* Clauses may also be combined with a subordinate conjunction such as *after, although, as, because, before, if, since, when, where, while, until, unless,* and so on.

EXAMPLES

Combining with a Relative Pronoun:
The writer is working on a new book. She has already published one book.
The writer, *who* has already published one book, is working on a new one.

Combining with a Subordinate Conjunction:
Carlos has started doing homework. He is getting better grades.
***Since* Carlos has started doing homework, he is getting better grades.**

Note: When you are combining simple sentences into complex sentences, you may find it necessary to change an independent clause to a dependent clause. Examine the sentences carefully to see which clause is more important; then you'll know which clause (the less important one) can be subordinated.

Directions   Combine each of the following pairs of sentences into one complex sentence. Refer to page 96 and to 438.1 in *Write Source 2000.*

Answers may vary.

1. The writer's first book wasn't very popular. She was not discouraged.

   Although the writer's first book wasn't very popular, she was not

   discouraged.

2. Yi had faith in her ability. She started a new book immediately.

   Because Yi had faith in her ability, she started a new book immediately.

All Write pp. 58 and 372

3. The publisher suggested that Yi write a book on her experiences in gymnastics. She had been an excellent gymnast.

   Because she had been an excellent gymnast, the publisher suggested

   that Yi write a book on her experiences in gymnastics.

4. She thought the new book would be easy to write. It was on a topic familiar to her.

   Because the new book was on a topic familiar to her, she thought it

   would be easy to write.

5. Yi felt comfortable writing about gymnastics. She had been a gymnast since age three.

   Yi, who had been a gymnast since age three, felt comfortable writing

   about gymnastics.

6. Yi researched the topic. She discovered that gymnastics had changed considerably.

   As Yi researched the topic, she discovered that gymnastics had

   changed considerably.

7. Yi has been working hard on her new book. She has not worried about her first book.

   Since Yi has been working hard on her new book, she has not

   worried about her first book.

8. The publishers mounted a nationwide promotional campaign. They sensed outstanding sales potential.

   Because they sensed outstanding sales potential, the publishers

   mounted a nationwide promotional campaign.

Next Step Write a paragraph about an experience you had persevering after a first attempt failed. Then combine some of the sentences into complex sentences. Use a variety of dependent clauses. Make sure that the most important clause remains the independent clause.

Sentence-Combining Review 1

Combining short, simple sentences into longer, more meaningful ones improves writing that sounds stiff and choppy. (Turn to pages 93-96 in *Write Source 2000* for more information.)

Directions Combine the following set of four short sentences into longer, smoother-reading ones. Follow the sentence "frames" when they are provided for you.

Shorter Sentences:
Jolene is an unusual girl.
She performs at school assemblies.
She recites from Webster's Collegiate Dictionary.
It is a book of 1,563 pages that she has memorized.

Frame 1: Jolene _____ *is an unusual* _____ girl

who _____ *performs at school assemblies* _____

by reciting _____ *from Webster's Collegiate Dictionary* _____ ,

a book _____ *of 1,563 pages that she has memorized* _____ .

Frame 2: Jolene, an unusual _____ *girl* _____ ,

performs _____ *at school assemblies* _____

by _____ *reciting from Webster's Collegiate Dictionary* _____ ,

a _____ *book of 1,563 pages that she has memorized* _____ .

Frame 3: (Come up with your own version.)

An unusual girl, Jolene, performs at school assemblies by reciting from a

1,563-page book that she has memorized—Webster's Collegiate Dictionary.

_____

_____

_____

All Write pp. 45 and 55-58

| | **Directions** | Combine the following sets of simple sentences and then, on your own paper, finish the story. The first combined sentence has been done for you. |

1. Jerri thought tryouts were easier last year. She was in sixth grade then.

Jerri thought tryouts were easier last year when she was in sixth grade.

2. She had thought for sure she had made the team. The coach had cut her.

She had thought for sure she had made the team, but the coach had cut her.

3. She had wondered if Coach Anderson liked her. He sometimes yelled at her.

She had wondered if Coach Anderson liked her, because he sometimes yelled at her.

4. Jerri now thinks something different. Maybe the coach was trying to help her.

Jerri now thinks that maybe the coach was trying to help her.

5. The practice lasted another 30 minutes. Coach Anderson stopped practice.

Coach Anderson stopped the practice after another 30 minutes.

6. He told the players to take a shower. He told them to check the board on their way out. A list of players who made the second cut would be posted.

He told them to take a shower and to check the board on their way out for a list of players who made the second cut.

7. Jerri headed for the showers. She . . . (*Finish this story on your own paper.*)

Next Step Write a story about a situation that made you anxious. Exchange stories with a classmate. Check each other's work for choppiness. Correct or combine the sentences as necessary.

Sentence-Combining Review 2

Directions Use sentence-combining techniques to make each set of shorter sentences below into one longer sentence. Use the method indicated in parentheses at the end of each sentence to combine the sentences. Place your responses in the spaces provided. (For more information about sentence-combining techniques, turn to pages 93-96 in *Write Source 2000*.)

1. Billy bowled three strikes. He bowled a split. **(Use a subordinate conjunction to make this a complex sentence.)**

   After Billy bowled three strikes, he bowled a split.

2. The match was long. The match was close. The match was exciting. **(Use a series of words.)**

   The match was long, close, and exciting.

3. Jess plays chess every day. Maria plays chess every day. **(Use a compound subject.)**

   Jess and Maria play chess every day.

4. I went to bed early. I couldn't fall asleep. **(Use a compound sentence.)**

   I went to bed early, but I couldn't fall asleep.

5. I always did my math homework. I still failed the exams. **(Use a compound verb.)**

   I always did my math homework and still failed the exams.

6. The officer asked us to move along. The officer smiled. **(Use the participle *smiling*.)**

   The smiling officer asked us to move along.

All Write pp. 48, 55-58, and 391

Directions Combine each of the following sets of simple sentences into one complex sentence on the lines provided. The first sentence has been done for you.

1. Dan's right eye was twitching. He sat waiting for the test paper.

   Dan's right eye was twitching as he sat waiting for the test paper.

2. This was the last big English test of the term. Dan couldn't afford to fail it.

   Because this was the last big English test of the term, Dan couldn't afford to fail it.

3. Dan had studied hard for the test. He still didn't feel confident.

   Although Dan had studied hard for the test, he still didn't feel confident.

4. Five minutes passed. Mr. Adams looked down Dan's row. He saw Dan just sitting there.

   After five minutes passed, Mr. Adams looked down Dan's row and saw him just sitting there.

5. Dan couldn't write a single line. His mind was a complete blank.

   Dan couldn't write a single line because his mind was a complete blank.

6. Mr. Adams got up from his chair. He walked down the aisle toward Dan.

   After Mr. Adams got up from his chair, he walked down the aisle toward Dan.

Next Step Complete the story on your own paper. Be ready to read aloud in class your startling conclusion to "The Testing of Dan."

Sentence Fragments 1

A sentence is more than a random collection of words and phrases, just as an airplane is more than a pile of parts and pieces. (Neither will "fly" with parts missing.) A sentence must contain a subject and a predicate (verb), which are arranged with other words to form a complete thought. A sentence that does not express a complete thought is called a **sentence fragment**. (Turn to page 86 in *Write Source 2000* for more information about fragments.)

EXAMPLES

Sentence Fragment:
Are slender and furry.
(A subject is missing.)

Complete Sentence:
Otters are slender and furry.
(A subject has been added.)

Sentence Fragment:
The furry otter.
(A verb is missing.)

Complete Sentence:
The furry otter is related to the weasel.
(A verb has been added.)

| Directions | Identify the following groups of words with an *S* for each sentence or an *F* for each fragment. The first one has been done for you. |

_F___ **1.** The otter's oily fur, which forms a waterproof coat.

_S___ **2.** River otters, once common in North America, are rarely seen.

_F___ **3.** Are afraid of humans.

_S___ **4.** Chattering noisily, they take turns sliding down snowy or muddy banks and belly flopping into the water.

_S___ **5.** Webbed toes and strong tails make otters excellent swimmers.

_F___ **6.** Paddling with their feet and using their strong tails to steer.

_F___ **7.** Prized for their rich fur like their relative the mink.

_S___ **8.** In the 1880's, otters were trapped heavily and began disappearing.

_F___ **9.** Are now a protected species with many programs to help them.

All Write p. 50

Sentence Fragments 2

A capital letter at the beginning of a group of words and a period at the end doesn't make a sentence. A sentence must contain a subject and a predicate and must express a complete thought. Sometimes, when you are writing rapidly, you might write a sentence fragment instead of the sentence you really wanted to write. Check what you write by editing carefully. If you discover you have written a fragment instead of a sentence, add the missing ingredients to make it a complete thought.

> **Directions**   Put an *F* in front of each sentence fragment below. Put an *S* in front of each sentence. The first two have been done for you. (For examples and explanations, turn to page 86 in *Write Source 2000*.)

_S_ **1.** Beetles are the largest group of insects in existence today.

_F_ **2.** More than 277,000 species around the world.

_F_ **3.** What amounts to two pairs of wings on every beetle.

_S_ **4.** A sheath on top helps protect beetles.

_F_ **5.** Thin flying wings underneath.

_S_ **6.** The larvae of some species, but not all, damage plants.

_S_ **7.** The potato beetle and boll weevil are important examples.

_S_ **8.** Fireflies, soft-bodied beetles, can light up the evening sky.

_F_ **9.** No wings on female fireflies.

_F_ **10.** Whirligigs, a type of aquatic beetle, found in lakes and ponds.

_F_ **11.** One set of eyes above and one below the waterline.

_F_ **12.** Diving beetles, which breathe under water.

_S_ **13.** Air bubbles are used for oxygen supply.

_S_ **14.** Have you heard of the *splendor* beetle that lived 47 years as a larva?

_F_ **15.** The heaviest insect in the world, the African goliath beetle, which can weigh 3-1/2 ounces.

Comma Splices and Run-Ons 1

A **comma splice** occurs when you incorrectly connect two simple sentences with a comma instead of a period, semicolon, or connecting word.

A **run-on sentence** occurs when you incorrectly join two simple sentences without using any punctuation. (A period, a semicolon, or a comma and a coordinating conjunction are ways of correcting run-ons.) Both comma splices and run-on sentences can be avoided if you carefully review each of your sentences before sharing your writing with your readers. (For more information, see pages 86-87 in *Write Source 2000*.)

EXAMPLES

Comma Splice:
Bamboo is a giant form of grass, its shoots are a tasty vegetable.

Run-On:
Bamboo is a giant form of grass its shoots are a tasty vegetable.

Corrected Sentences:
Bamboo is a giant form of grass. Its shoots are a tasty vegetable. *Or* . . .
Bamboo is a giant form of grass, *and* its shoots are a tasty vegetable.

Directions

Place a *CS* in front of each comma splice, an *RO* in front of each run-on sentence, and a *C* in front of each correct sentence. Correct each faulty sentence. The first sentence has been done for you. *Answers may vary.*

<u>CS</u> **1.** Bamboo is definitely one of the most interesting plants, *and* it is

valued for its beauty and usefulness.

<u>C</u> **2.** Bamboo may be one of the world's most useful plants.

<u>RO</u> **3.** Bamboo grows in huge groves. it serves as a natural buffer

against floods, erosion, and earthquake shocks.

<u>C</u> **4.** In addition, bamboo enriches the soil.

All Write p. 50

_RO_ 5. People have found bamboo indispensable, they use it for buildings,

for musical instruments, and for furniture.

_CS_ 6. Bamboo is also an important food source, its crisp texture makes

it a favorite ingredient in Asian cooking.

_C_ 7. Bamboo is interesting not only to ordinary people, but it is also

interesting to scientists.

_RO_ 8. This plant is a member of the grass family. it grows naturally on

every continent except Europe and Antarctica.

_C_ 9. About a thousand different species of bamboo exist, differing

widely in color, shape, and size.

_CS_ 10. Bamboo varies greatly in size, some varieties grow to the height

of field grass while others reach heights of more than 100 feet.

_C_ 11. All bamboo plants have stalks known as _culms_.

_CS_ 12. The culm is usually round, hollow, and jointed, it makes the

plant unusually strong.

_RO_ 13. One of the most interesting features of bamboo is its growth

speed. nothing grows as tall and as rapidly as bamboo.

_C_ 14. In Japan, a common type of bamboo is known to have grown

four feet in 24 hours.

_RO_ 15. At this rate, the stalk's growth would likely be visible. an

observer, however, would have to be extremely patient.

Next Step Sometimes it's easier to catch sentence errors in someone else's writing than in your own. (You are, in a sense, too close to your own work.) Exchange a piece of writing in progress with a classmate and check each other's work for comma splices and run-on sentences.

Comma Splices and Run-Ons 2

Combining several related thoughts into the same sentence can be a good thing. You just need to avoid two pitfalls: **run-on sentences** and **comma splices.** Enthusiastic or fast writers often make these errors in their early drafts, but careful editing can catch these errors. Experiment with different punctuation—periods, semicolons—and different connecting words—*and, but, nor, or, yet, for*—to get the effect you want. (Refer to pages 86-87 in *Write Source 2000* for more information.)

EXAMPLES

Incorrect:
He swung at the ball, he missed it.

Correct:
He swung at the ball; he missed it.
He swung at the ball, *but* he missed it.
He swung at the ball. He missed it.

| **Directions** | In the groups of words below, place a *CS* before each comma splice and an *RO* before each run-on sentence. Then correct each error. If a sentence is correct, place a *C* before the sentence. The first one has been done for you. *Answers may vary.* |

<u> CS </u> **1.** Some people are afraid of spiders; other people think they are a sign of good luck.

<u> RO </u> **2.** Most spiders are strange-looking creatures, *but* they aren't harmful.

<u> RO </u> **3.** Spiders are often used in monster films; these spiders are huge.

<u> CS </u> **4.** Spiders have eight eyes; they have eight mouths, too.

<u> RO </u> **5.** Spiders use their mouths to eat. Most have poisonous fangs to paralyze their prey.

All Write p. 50

_____C_____ **6.** Not every spider spins webs, but each one has spinnerets, which allows it to spin fine silk threads.

_____RO_____ **7.** Silk is used by different types of spiders for different things, it can be used for webs and for wrapping victims.

_____C_____ **8.** Baby spiders of some species (called "parachuters") spin long thin threads and are carried away by the wind, scattering over a wide area.

_____RO_____ **9.** The trap-door spider actually makes a hinged door, it digs a hole in the ground and closes the door over the hole.

_____C_____ **10.** The California trap-door spider is so strong that it can resist a force 38 times its weight.

_____CS_____ **11.** Black widow spiders can actually be deadly, their bites can cause illness and sometimes even death to humans.

_____CS_____ **12.** The most venomous spider is the Brazilian huntsman, it often hides in people's shoes.

_____RO_____ **13.** The largest spider ever found had a leg span of 11 inches, the smallest spider was the size of a period on this page.

_____C_____ **14.** Why do some spiders buzz and others purr?

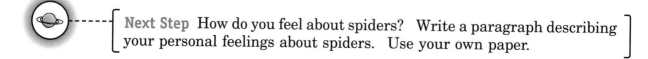

Next Step How do you feel about spiders? Write a paragraph describing your personal feelings about spiders. Use your own paper.

Sentence Errors Review 1

Good sentences are essential to good writing. In order to write good sentences, you need to avoid some basic sentence errors. Three of the more common sentence errors are **run-on sentences, comma splices,** and **sentence fragments.** (Refer to your *Write Source 2000* handbook pages 86-87 to review these errors, or look back to specific exercises you have already completed on each type of error.)

| **Directions** | Place an *RO* in front of each run-on sentence that follows. Place a *CS* in front of each comma splice and an *F* before each sentence fragment. Then fix each error. The first one has been done for you. *Answers may vary.* |

___*RO*___ **1.** Last night, Sam and I biked to the arena to see Garbage in

concert‸it was a very interesting ride.
        ;

was congested
___*F*___ **2.** Our route through downtown traffic‸.

___*CS*___ **3.** Biking soon became tricky‸the roads were jammed with traffic
              ;

heading for the concert.

           were
___*F*___ **4.** Impatient drivers‸blowing their car horns.

___*CS*___ **5.** Sam was really nervous about all the traffic‸he wasn't used to
                   ;

bumper-to-bumper cars.

   The traffic was
___*F*___ **6.** ‸More like New York City than Madison, Wisconsin.

                            C
___*CS*___ **7.** We were riding in the bike lane‸cars kept edging over toward

us.

___*RO*___ **8.** We finally made it to the arena⊙Sam confessed he had been

worried we wouldn't make it.

   We were
___*F*___ **9.** ‸Sitting so far back that the musicians looked like ants.

                             W
___*RO*___ **10.** The sound was great, though⊙we probably heard better than

the people in the front row.

       All Write p. 50

Sentence Errors Review 2

Directions Put an *RO* in front of any run-on sentences that follow, a *CS* in front of any comma splices, and an *F* in front of any fragments. Then fix each error. (Refer to pages 86-87 in your *Write Source 2000* handbook for explanations and examples.)

Answers may vary.

CS 1. My dad is a long-time member of our town's volunteer fire department, *(or) ; H* he also belongs to our local rescue squad.

F 2. *He is* Always getting called to a fire or accident right in the middle of supper or when his favorite football team is playing on television.

RO 3. One night he rescued two kittens from a burning barn and brought them home. *W* we named the kittens Sparky and Soot.

F 4. *We* Still have both kittens 10 years later.

CS 5. The kittens are all grown up now, *T* they have become regular members of our family.

RO 6. I'll never forget the night we got Sparky and Soot, *(or) ; T* they were cold and smelled like smoke.

F 7. Tiny heads *were* poking out of the pockets of my dad's big rubber coat.

CS 8. I thought they were toys, *then* I heard them meow.

F 9. For a child, *are* there many things cuter than baby kittens?

RO 10. My sister and I loved the kittens *(or) ; W* we took them up in our treehouse and everywhere we went.

Rambling Sentences

Just as you should correct any fragments, run-ons, or comma splices in your writing, you should also be careful not to use too many *and*'s or *but*'s. The result could be a series of rambling sentences. (Turn to page 87 in *Write Source 2000* for more information.)

Answers may vary.

Directions	In the following passage (a rewritten scene from *The Adventures of Tom Sawyer* by Mark Twain), look for sentences that ramble on and on. Fix them by taking out some (but not all) of the *and*'s, *but*'s, or *so*'s. Also, add punctuation and capitalization as needed.

1 Tom typically carried treasures in his pocket, but this particular

2 Sunday, the "pinch bug" (a large black beetle with formidable jaws) was

3 taken out and the beetle helped himself to Tom's finger and was thereby

4 flicked into the church aisle but a poodle, in church with his master,

5 saw the bug, came up to it, and started to play with it and the poodle's

6 chin got too close and the chin was seized, there was a yelp, and the

7 pinch bug went flying farther down the aisle so the poodle moved

8 toward the beetle, became distracted by a fly, forgot about the beetle

9 entirely and sat down on it and with a wild yelp, the dog went

10 streaking up the aisle like a woolly comet. In desperation, the dog

11 jumped on his master's lap and was flung out of a nearby window and

12 people snickered, the sermon ended, and Tom went home quite satisfied

13 except for one thing he didn't mind that the dog had played with his

14 pinch bug but he did not think it right of the dog to carry it off.

- - - - - **Next Step** Write a paragraph about a memorable animal experience. Exchange first drafts with a classmate. Check each other's writing for any rambling sentences and checkmark those sentences that need to be rewritten. Return the papers and make corrections as necessary.

All Write p. 50

Wordiness

In a popular book about writing entitled *Elements of Style*, the authors stress the importance of simplicity. They explain that you achieve simplicity in writing by removing unnecessary words or phrases.

EXAMPLE

Wordy Sentence:

I kept thinking about all the things I needed to remember to take along for tomorrow's fishing trip—my lures, the rods, the bait.

Clearer Sentence:

I kept thinking about everything I needed for tomorrow's trip—my lures, rods, bait.

> **Directions** Read the model paragraph and cross out any words that you think are unnecessary. (Some sentences can be corrected in more than one way.) *Answers may vary.*

(1) It was late—time to go to sleep if we wanted to get up ~~early~~ at 4:00 a.m. ~~in the morning~~ for some good fishing. (2) But we needed worms and were too excited to sleep ~~which goes without saying~~. (3) We carefully slid the patio door open ~~with great care~~, trying hard to keep quiet ~~and not make any noise either~~. (4) There was a light fog that seemed to cling to everything ~~it touched~~. (5) Closing the door slowly, we stepped softly onto the patio. (6) My friend~~, he~~ turned on his flashlight ~~so we could see better in the haze~~. (7) We found the worm box on the garage shelf and headed for the flower garden~~, walking toward it from the garage~~. (8) I flashed my flashlight at the moist ground and spotted a couple of fat night crawlers slipping back into their holes ~~and sliding under the ground to escape~~. (9) My friend grabbed them just in time and dropped them into the box. (10) On we went, shining our lights and grabbing worms until we had plenty of bait ~~that would be enough~~ for a morning of fishing. (11) ~~My friend and I,~~ W~~w~~e were tired as we put everything away and sneaked back to our room, finally ready to get some rest before our fishing trip.

Next Step Check at least one of your most recent writings and eliminate any unnecessary words you may have included.

Sentence Expanding

Good writers have a knack for wording things the right way. They expand ideas with words and phrases that make their writing work. The smooth flow of their thoughts makes the actual words and sentences almost invisible. (Turn to pages 129-136 in *Write Source 2000* for more examples.)

EXAMPLES

Details Added After the Basic Sentence:
<u>He looks different</u>, *a little less like camp, a little more dressed up.*
                              From *There's a Bat in Bunk Five* by Paula Danziger

<u>Wil nodded to himself and slipped away</u>, *softly as a mouse, toward the back of the house where the tourists were never taken.*
                              From "A Room Full of Leaves" by Joan Aiken

Details Added Before the Basic Sentence:
If his surroundings were gloomy and the company either boring to him or nonexistent, <u>he did not fidget.</u>
                              From "Total Stranger" by James Gould Cozzens

Details Added Before and After the Basic Sentence:
At the first sign of alarm, <u>he saw them clamber down the sapling and slip away</u> *to the west beyond the gullberries.*
                              From *The Yearling* by Marjorie Kinnan Rawlings

From then on, <u>it was like they were two dogs</u>, *each waiting for the other one to make a move and start the fight.*
                              From *Hoops* by Walter Dean Meyers

Directions Study the sentences above. Read them out loud or have a partner read them to you. Listen carefully. Choose the two sentences you like best. On a separate piece of paper, write your own sentences, modeled after the professional writers' sentences. (To see how this is done, check out the example on page 133 in your *Write Source 2000* handbook under "Modeling Sentences.")

All Write pp. 87-94

Directions Expand the three basic sentences that follow into longer, more meaningful thoughts.

1. Connie began to laugh.

In spite of the seriousness of the situation, Connie began to laugh, at first to herself, then more and more loudly.

2. Charles turned quickly.

Anticipating the behind-the-back pass, Charles turned quickly to intercept it.

3. Lakesha found the answer.

After hours of exhausting research in the library and on the Internet, Lakesha found the answer to one of life's most perplexing problems.

Next Step Refer to one of the short stories you've read in class, an article in your favorite magazine, or a section in one of your favorite books and copy down two expanded sentences that you really like. Underline the basic sentence and circle the words, phrases, and clauses that were used to expand it. Compare your findings with those of a classmate.

Editing for Clarity 1

Directions   Read the paragraph below. It contains a number of words, phrases, and sentences that are unclear and could easily mislead the reader. Find one example of each type of error listed beneath the paragraph; write the number of the sentence in which you found each error on the blank provided. (Turn to pages 88-92 in *Write Source 2000* for help.)   Then correct each error in the paragraph itself.   (Rewrite the one sentence that needs major revising on the lines provided.)

(1) Learning to pilot a Superflooz VII Intergalactic Spacezipper at ultralight speed is really much easier than it sounds. (2) First, the pilot must strap into the control seat so he or she ~~can't~~ *can* hardly move. (3) Then he *or she* must switch on the viewing screen. (4) This special screen ~~nearly~~ allows the pilot to see for *nearly* five miles. (5) At this point, the pilot must switch on the Magno-Zip Atombooster.   (6) This switch is located just above the pilot's head and looks sort of like a radish. (7) One of the switches ~~are~~ *is* green and should not be touched at all, for it will activate the ship's destruct mechanism. (8) ~~After warming up for three minutes, the pilot can throw the switch for the Magno-Zip Atombooster to the no-return position.~~ (9) The pilot must remember not to overload ~~their~~ *his or her* Magno-Zip Atombooster. (10) If ~~he~~ *the pilot* follows ~~one~~ *all* of these directions carefully, ~~it~~ *the trip* should be a smooth one.

__2__ Double negative		__3, 9__ Pronoun problem (agreement)	
__4__ Misplaced modifier (one word)		__8__ Misplaced modifier (phrase)	
__7__ Agreement of subject and verb		__10__ Confusing pronoun reference	

Revised Sentence: *(8) After warming up the Magno-Zip Atombooster for three minutes, the pilot can throw the switch to the no-return position.*

All Write pp. 51-54

Editing for Clarity 2

All writing should read smoothly and move clearly (logically) from one point to the next. Transitional or linking words like *also, finally,* and *later* and the repetition of key words or phrases can help make your writing smooth reading and clear. (Turn to page 106 in *Write Source 2000* for a list of many different linking words.)

Directions — Many of the linking words have been taken out of the paragraph below. Read the paragraph and fill in each blank with a linking word or expression that helps the paragraph flow smoothly from one point to the next. Share your results.

1   When I was younger, I was always begging my parents to let me cook

2 something by myself. _____*Finally*_____, my father said he'd teach

3 me how to fry an egg. What a mess! _____*First*_____, we got out all

4 the dishes and utensils we needed—frying pan, pot holder, spatula, cup,

5 plate, and fork. _____*Then*_____, we got the eggs and margarine

6 from the refrigerator. _____*After*_____ accidentally smashing one egg

7 on the floor and letting another roll into the sink, I finally managed to crack

8 an egg into the cup and throw the shell into the garbage. _____*Next*_____, I

9 heated a little margarine in the frying pan and slowly poured the egg from

10 the cup into the pan. Flipping the egg over when it was done on one side

11 was the hardest part. Melted margarine sure splatters. _____*Also*_____,

12 when it was time to lift my breakfast out of the pan, I discovered how

13 slippery fried eggs are. _____*After*_____ a few tries, I did manage to

14 slide my over-easy egg onto the plate, but there was nothing easy about it.

15 _____*Finally*_____, it was time to eat. _____*Even though*_____ cooking was

16 more work than I had expected, that egg tasted great!

Language Activities

Every activity includes a main practice section in which you learn about or review the different parts of speech. Most of the activities include helpful handbook references. In addition, the **Next Step** activities give you follow-up practice with certain skills.

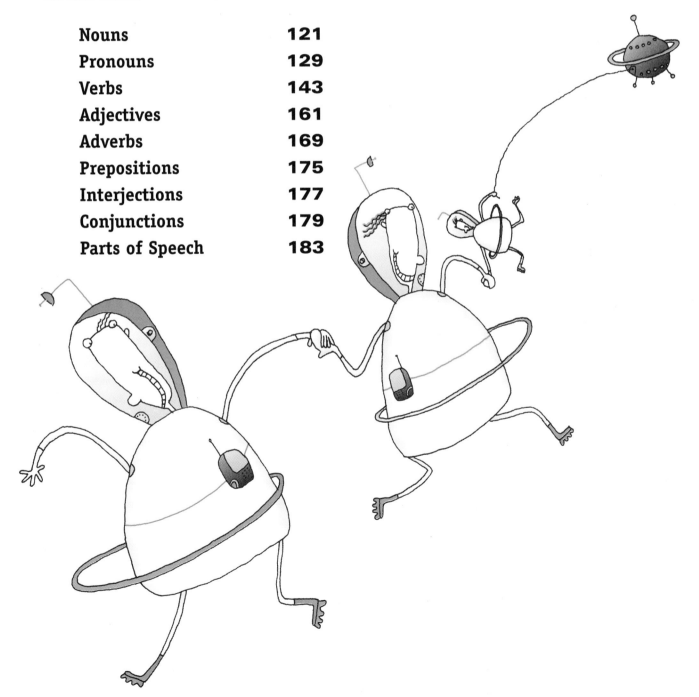

Common and Proper Nouns

A noun names a person, a place, a thing, or an idea. A **common noun** names any one of a group—not a specific person, place, thing, or idea. A common noun is *not* capitalized. A **proper noun** names a specific person, place, thing or idea. A proper noun is capitalized. (Turn to 439.1-439.2 in *Write Source 2000* for more information.)

EXAMPLES

Common Nouns	Proper Nouns
man	José
book	*American Heritage Dictionary*
city	Baltimore
team	Chicago Cubs

Directions Underline the nouns in the sentences that follow. Write *C* above each common noun and *P* above each proper noun. The first sentence has been done for you.

1. The words in our language have been put into eight groups called the parts of speech.
   C   C   C   C   C

2. A noun is the part of speech that names a person, a place, a thing, or an idea.
   C   C   C   C   C   C   C

3. Common nouns name common things: roads, cars, teams, and so on.
   C   C   C   C   C

4. Proper nouns are more specific: Avery Road, Ford, and New York Yankees.
   C   P   P   P

5. Can you pick the proper nouns out of this list: Saturn, meteor, rainbow, Apollo, John Glenn, Labor Day?
   *C   C   P   C   C
    P   P   P*

6. Remember, common nouns name common things and are not capitalized; proper nouns name specific things and are capitalized.
   *C   C
    C   C*

All Write p. 375

Directions Study the two lists of nouns that follow. Then add three nouns to each list. Make sure your nouns fit with the rest of the words in each list. *Answers will vary.*

clock   Big Ben
book   *Gentle Ben*
car   Volkswagen
group   Eagles

_____   _____

_____   _____

_____   _____

Directions On the lines provided below, explain the difference between the nouns in the two lists above. *Answers will vary.*

The nouns in the first list are common nouns—they do not name a

specific person, place, thing, or idea. The nouns in the second list are

proper nouns—they name a specific person, place, thing, or idea.

_____

_____

Note: Share your explanation with one of your classmates. Then compare it with the explanations in *Write Source 2000* at 439.1 and 439.2. How close does your explanation match the one in the handbook?

Next Step Select one noun from the first list at the top of this page (*clock* through *group*) as the beginning of a concrete poem or a title-down poem. (See pages 206-207 in *Write Source 2000* for help with your poem.)

Concrete and Abstract Nouns

Ask my brother to wash dishes, and he'll answer, "Get real!" Actually, dirty dishes are "real" enough. You can see them, feel them—maybe even smell them! **Concrete nouns** name physical things like those dishes. But what if you can't see or touch something? Is love "real"? Of course it is. **Abstract nouns,** such as "love" and "poverty," name things that you can think about but can't see or touch. (Turn to 439.3 and 439.4 in *Write Source 2000* for more information.)

Directions	Underline the nouns in the sentences that follow. Then put a *C* above each concrete noun and an *A* above each abstract noun. Some words are tricky! They may name either a concrete or an abstract concept. The first sentence has been done for you.

1. When we gaze at <u>stars</u> *(C)*, we are looking into the distant <u>past</u> *(A)*, because the <u>light</u> *(C)* from <u>stars</u> *(C)* takes many <u>years</u> *(A)* to travel to <u>Earth</u> *(C)*.

2. Some <u>dinosaurs</u> *(C)* half-buried their <u>eggs</u> *(C)* in <u>mud</u> *(C)*, then covered the <u>tops</u> *(C)* with rotting <u>vegetation</u> *(C)* to warm them.

3. It is an amazing <u>fact</u> *(A)* that giant <u>redwoods</u> *(C)* transport <u>water</u> *(C)* tremendous <u>distances</u> *(A)* from their <u>roots</u> *(C)* to their <u>leaves</u> *(C)* without a <u>pump</u> *(C)*.

4. By performing a <u>dance</u> *(C)*, a <u>honeybee</u> *(C)* can tell other <u>workers</u> *(C)* in the <u>hive</u> *(C)* where <u>flowers</u> *(C)* filled with <u>nectar</u> *(C)* can be found.

5. <u>Hummingbirds</u> *(C)* are not shy; if you wear red <u>clothes</u> *(C)*, they will fly close enough to get a careful <u>look</u> *(A)* at you.

6. The <u>Constitution</u> *(C)* guarantees all <u>Americans</u> *(C)* basic <u>freedoms</u> *(A)*.

7. It was not easy for the original 13 <u>colonies</u> *(C)* to win those <u>freedoms</u> *(A)*.

8. In fact, many <u>colonists</u> *(C)* did not like the <u>idea</u> *(A)* of a <u>rebellion</u> *(A)* against <u>England</u> *(C)*.

All Write p. 375

$\overset{A}{\qquad} \overset{C}{\qquad}$

9. Some continued to declare their loyalty to King George.

$\overset{C}{\qquad} \overset{C}{\qquad} \overset{C}{\qquad}$

10. The Eiffel Tower reminds me of drawings in my geometry book.

$\overset{C}{\qquad} \overset{C}{\qquad} \overset{C}{\qquad}$

11. At the basketball game, one of the players had to leave the game because of

$\overset{A}{\qquad}$

an injury.

$\overset{C}{\qquad} \overset{C}{\qquad}$

12. He sprained his ankle when he stepped on someone else's foot.

$\overset{C}{\qquad} \overset{A}{\qquad} \overset{C}{\qquad}$

13. The teams showed good sportsmanship even when the spectators were a

little rude.

$\overset{C}{\qquad} \overset{A}{\qquad} \overset{A}{\qquad}$

14. Emilio went through a growth spurt last year.

$\overset{A}{\qquad} \overset{C}{\qquad} \overset{C}{\qquad}$

15. Now his dream is to play football in high school.

Next Step Share the results of your work with a classmate. Discuss any differences you may find. Talk about ways you can distinguish between abstract and concrete nouns, and write your guidelines in the space below.

_____

_____

_____

_____

Subject and Object Nouns

Every word in a sentence has a job to do. Nouns do more than just *name* a person, a place, a thing, or an idea. The specific job a noun does in a sentence depends on where it is used and how it is related to the other words. (Turn to 440.5-441.3 in *Write Source 2000*.)

EXAMPLES

Subject Noun:
Our *family* loved spending afternoons in the park.
(A *subject noun* names the person, place, thing, or idea that is doing the action or is being talked about: *family* is a subject noun.)

Predicate Noun:
Our favorite game was *football*.
(A *predicate noun* follows a linking verb or a form of the *be* verb—*is, are, was, were*—and repeats or renames the subject: *football* renames *game*.)

Object Noun:
We would often eat our *lunch* there.
(A noun becomes an *object noun* when it is used as the direct object, indirect object, or object of the preposition: *lunch* is a direct object.)

Possessive Noun:
My *family's* favorite lunch was pizza.
(A *possessive noun* is a noun that shows ownership: *family's* is a possessive noun.)

Directions
Label each underlined noun in the following sentences. Use *SN* for subject noun, *PN* for predicate noun, *POS* for possessive noun, *ON* for object noun. The first two sentences have been done for you.

SN 1. The small <u>park</u> in my neighborhood used to be my favorite place.

ON 2. My mother took me to the <u>park</u> almost every day.

ON 3. I chased <u>squirrels</u> and <u>pigeons</u> around the huge trees.

ON 4. My mother gave me <u>ice cream</u> and other treats.

POS 5. Kids from all over the <u>city's</u> south side gathered in the park.

All Write p. 378

_SN_ **6.** Parents sat and talked on benches while the <u>kids</u> played on the equipment.

_ON_ **7.** Old people came and played <u>chess</u> and checkers on stone tables in the sun.

_SN_ **8.** City police <u>officers</u> patrolled the park on their bicycles.

_PN_ **9.** The police officers were <u>part</u> of the fun.

_ON_ **10.** One police officer even gave me an ice-cream <u>cone</u>.

_SN_ **11.** Last summer many city <u>workers</u> went on strike.

_PN_ **12.** In just a few days, the park was a total <u>disaster</u>.

_ON_ **13.** People discarded <u>paper</u> and litter on the grass and playground.

_SN_ **14.** <u>Parents</u> didn't want their kids playing in a bunch of garbage.

POS **15.** The park had been a green oasis in the <u>city's</u> concrete desert.

_ON_ **16.** Neighborhood residents organized a clean-up-the-park <u>campaign</u>.

_SN_ **17.** On the designated day, practically the whole <u>neighborhood</u> showed up for work.

_ON_ **18.** People swept, raked, and picked up all the <u>garbage</u> in the park.

POS **19.** Four ladies from our building planted flowers along the <u>park's</u> walkway.

_PN_ **20.** The park was once again a wonderful <u>place</u> for everyone to enjoy.

Next Step Write a paragraph describing a time when people joined together to accomplish something. It might be a neighborhood project or something done in school. Where the activity took place doesn't really matter. What matters is that you describe something that people thought needed to be done and got together to do it. You might even want to write about something that you did with members of your own family.

Specific Nouns

Specific nouns are especially helpful when you are trying to create a clear image or word picture for a reader. Notice the difference between the two example sentences below. The first sentence contains general nouns, and it doesn't express a very clear idea. The second sentence, which includes more specific nouns, does express a clear idea. (Turn to page 135 in *Write Source 2000* for more information.)

The *scientist* wanted to study *animals* in another *country*.   (**general** nouns)

Jane Goodall wanted to study *chimpanzees* in *Tanzania*.   (**specific** nouns)

Look at the examples below. Notice that the nouns move from very general at the top to very specific at the bottom. By using a good number of specific nouns in your writing, you will make it easier for the reader to understand exactly what you are saying.

EXAMPLES

person	place	thing	idea
man	building	book	pain
artist	arena	reference book	headache
Vincent van Gogh	Madison Square Garden	Farmers' Almanac	migraine

Directions   Now think of three nouns for each of the categories below. Each noun you add must be more specific than the one before it as in the examples above.   *Answers will vary.*

person	place	thing	idea

EXAMPLE

The <u>car</u> drove past the <u>building</u>.

a. *The foreign car drove past the government building.*

b. *The Toyota convertible drove past the White House.*

Directions   Revise each of the following sentences twice. Make sentence B even more specific than sentence A. (Add or change other words as necessary to create a better sentence.)

Answers will vary.

1. The **animal** is in the **building**.

a. *The dog is in the kennel.*

b. *The German shepherd is in Brownsville Animal Shelter.*

2. The **doctor** performed the **operation**.

a. *The specialist performed the heart surgery.*

b. *The cardiologist performed the bypass surgery.*

3. The **singer** was given an **award**.

a. *The pop singer was given a trophy.*

b. *Celine Dion was given a Grammy.*

4. A **relative** came down with an **illness**.

a. *My sister came down with the measles.*

b. *My sister Joan came down with the German measles.*

5. The **dog** ran around the **tree**.

a. *The terrier ran around the oak tree.*

b. *The Irish terrier ran around the dead oak tree.*

(7)

Pronouns and Antecedents

You always want to write so your readers clearly understand what it is you're trying to say. The writer of the following sentence obviously wasn't careful or clear in what he or she said. (Taken from *Anguished English* by Richard Lederer.)

> About two years ago, a wart appeared on my left hand, which I wanted removed.

Make sure that the antecedent of a pronoun (the word the pronoun refers to) is always clear in your writing. (For more information, turn to 441.4 in *Write Source 2000.*)

EXAMPLES

Unclear Pronoun Use:

I took my car to the corner gas station because it was nearly empty.
(This sentence does not clearly state *what* was nearly empty—the car or the gas station—because the antecedent of the pronoun *it* is unclear.)

Clear Pronoun and Antecedent:

Because my *car* was nearly empty, I took *it* to the corner gas station.
(*Car* is definitely the antecedent of the pronoun *it* in this sentence.)

Directions	Rewrite each of the following sentences so that the pronoun has a clearly stated antecedent. Be sure to use the boldfaced pronoun in your new sentence. The first sentence has been done for you. *Answers may vary.*

1. Reggie sat in the first row of the theater since **it** was empty.

   Since the first row of the theater was empty, Reggie sat in it.

2. When I put my foot into the shoe, **it** was wet.

   My foot was wet when I put it into the shoe.

All Write p. 379

3. When the ice floe reached the old dam, **it** broke.

The ice floe broke when it reached the old dam.

4. After he'd left the present on the doorstep, Gerard realized **it** was the wrong one.

Gerald realized it was the wrong present after he'd left it on the

doorstep.

5. Though the chauffeur drove the limousine into the fence, **it** wasn't damaged.

The limousine wasn't damaged even though the chauffeur drove it

into the fence.

6. I can't feed the hot dog to my dog because **it** is too old.

Because the hot dog is too old, I can't feed it to my dog.

7. I don't go to movies with my young cousins because **they** are too violent. (_they_ becomes _them_)

Because movies are too violent, I don't go to them with my young

cousins.

8. Traffic, on the way to my aunt's dinner, **which** was terrible, made us late.

Traffic, which was terrible on the way to my aunt's dinner, made us

late.

Next Step Turn to page 443 in _Write Source 2000_ to find a chart of singular and plural personal pronouns. Study it carefully! Then close your book and see how many of the pronouns you can list. Check your list against the one in your handbook.

Person and Number of a Pronoun

The **person** of a pronoun tells whether a pronoun is the speaker in a sentence (first person = *I*, *we*, etc.), the person being spoken to (second person = *you*), or the person or thing being talked about (third person = *he*, *it*, *they*, etc.).

The **number** of a pronoun tells whether a pronoun is singular or plural. The number of a pronoun and its noun (antecedent) must match. (For more information, turn to 442.2-442.5 in *Write Source 2000*.)

EXAMPLES

Singular Pronoun:
A monarch butterfly must spend *its* winter in a warm climate.

Plural Pronoun:
In late August, *monarch butterflies* begin *their* southern migration.

| Directions | Circle the pronoun that completes each sentence below. The first sentence has been done for you. |

1. When asters and goldenrod bloom, *(it,* (they)*)* signal that monarchs are on the move.

2. An organization called Monarch Watch involves thousands of volunteers in *(*(its,)* their)* tagging and logging of the butterflies.

3. The volunteers gently capture the monarchs and tag *(it,* (them)*)*.

4. The volunteers then fill in data sheets and send *(it,* (them)*)* to university research centers.

5. Environmentalists want to know whether monarchs follow a path or simply travel in a particular direction as *(it,* (they)*)* move across the continent.

All Write pp. 379-380

6. *((They,)* *You)* hope to learn whether migration is the same from year to year, and how weather affects the butterflies.

7. Monarch Watch volunteers are often teachers and students who conduct research as part of *((their,)* *our)* science classes.

8. Using a good butterfly net, a student captures *((his or her,)* *their)* butterfly, then holds *(them,* *(it))* gently while applying a self-sticking tag.

9. A butterfly is tagged on a cell under *(his,* *(its))* hind wing.

10. The mitten-shaped cell is near a butterfly's center of gravity, where the sticker application doesn't restrict *(their,* *(its))* flight.

11. Before each butterfly is released, *(their,* *(its))* tag number, sex, appearance, and other information are noted on a data sheet.

12. Second graders are some of the best taggers, because *((they,)* *he)* can apply the self-sticking tags with *((their,)* *his)* smaller fingertips!

13. The more kids know about butterflies, the better *(we,* *(they))* will understand the connections among all living things.

14. Eastern monarchs travel to forest sites in central Mexico, where 40 million of *(they,* *(them))* roost at a site that's open to the public.

15. *((You,)* *They)* can see western monarchs in smaller, temporary sites from Mendocino, California, to the Ensenada region of Baja California Sur.

Uses of Pronouns

Just like the nouns they replace, pronouns can be subjects or objects in a sentence. Possessive pronouns can also stand in for possessive nouns. Most of the time, using the correct form of the pronoun isn't a problem. But sometimes, substituting a pronoun for a noun can result in confusion.

As you review the examples below, you'll notice that many problems with pronouns happen because people write the way they talk. (Turn to 442.6-443.2 and page 90 in *Write Source 2000* for more information.)

EXAMPLES

Incorrect:

Everyone has *their* own ticket.
(*Their* is plural and does not match its singular antecedent, *everyone*.)

Correct:

Everyone has *his or her* own ticket.
(*His or her* is singular. It now matches its singular antecedent, *everyone*.)
Note: When it's not clear if the pronoun should be male or female, use the phrase *his or her.*

Incorrect:

When Joan and Sharone were neighbors, *she* souped up *her* BMX bike.

Correct:

When Joan was Sharone's neighbor, she souped up Sharone's BMX bike.

Incorrect:

If someone sprains a knee, *you* will need physical therapy.
(*Someone* is a third-person subject. *You* is a second-person subject. The pronouns need to be in the same person or else it is not clear whose knee is sprained.)

Correct:

If someone sprains a knee, *he or she* will need physical therapy.

Incorrect:

John *he* makes great chili.
(Avoid using a pronoun immediately following a noun.)

Correct:

John makes great chili.

All Write pp. 53, 54, and 381

Directions   Correct the common pronoun errors in the sentences below by rewriting the sentences in the spaces provided. Be prepared to discuss why you made the corrections. The first sentence has been done for you.

1. Sue's dog, Voltaire, he likes to play soccer, but they often play too rough.

   Sue's dog, Voltaire, likes to play soccer, but he often plays too rough.

2. I don't suppose you thought about a person's feelings when you took my sweater and stretched it out, and then gave it back to that person without having it cleaned.

   I don't suppose you thought about my feelings when you took my

   sweater and stretched it out, and then gave it back to me without

   having it cleaned.

3. Soon, if an athlete injures their knee, doctors will be able to repair the sinews with a synthetic material that is twice as strong as their original muscle.

   Soon, if an athlete injures his or her knee, doctors will be able to repair

   the sinews with a synthetic material that is twice as strong as his or

   her original muscle.

4. If a student wants to participate in extracurricular sports, you have to maintain a passing grade-point average.

   If a student wants to participate in extracurricular sports, he or she

   has to maintain a passing grade-point average.

Next Step In one of the books you are reading, find a paragraph that uses a number of pronouns. Then list the pronouns on a sheet of paper and identify each one as either (1) a subject pronoun, (2) an object pronoun, or (3) a possessive pronoun. If you find an odd use that doesn't seem to fit the basic rules, ask your teacher for help.

Types of Pronouns 1

Pronouns do a great job of standing in for nouns. But some pronouns do more: *Reflexive* and *intensive* pronouns, for example, give their antecedents extra emphasis.

Another group of pronouns—*indefinite pronouns*—also stand in for nouns, but they don't refer to a definite person or thing. Indefinite pronouns are often used without antecedents. Indefinite pronouns keep the subject vague—which might be a relief to the person who is the subject: *Somebody* spilled the cereal. *Nobody* cleaned it up. *Somebody* left the bike in the driveway. (Turn to 444.4-445.3 in *Write Source 2000* for more information.)

EXAMPLES

Reflexive Pronoun:
Little Jeff has finally learned how to dress *himself*.
(The reflexive pronoun *himself* throws the action back on the subject of the sentence. The sentence would not be complete without it.)

Intensive Pronoun:
Little Jeff *himself* put on his pants.
(The intensive pronoun *himself* intensifies or emphasizes its antecedent. However, it's not necessary; the sentence is complete without it.)

Indefinite Pronoun:
Somebody left these pants on the floor.
(The indefinite pronoun *somebody* doesn't stand in for a particular person. The person is indefinite or unknown.)

Directions Write a reflexive, intensive, or indefinite pronoun in the blanks in the sentences below. Write *Ref* above each reflexive pronoun, *Int* above each intensive pronoun, and *Ind* above each indefinite pronoun. The first sentence has been done for you.

1. _____ *Ind* _____
   Something warned me not to make a sound as I tiptoed up the

   dark staircase.

2. Instead, I ended up making loud creaking sounds as if King Kong
   _____ *Int* _____
   himself were stomping up to the second story.

All Write p. 382

3. I could not stop _____ *Ref* *myself* _____ from trembling like a leaf.

4. As I reached the top of the stairs, I felt _____ *Ind* *something* _____ brush my

   leg, and then I heard it throw _____ *Ref* *itself* _____ down the stairs.

5. I stood as if frozen to the landing, desperately telling _____ *Ref* *myself* _____

   to calm down.

6. As my eyes adjusted to the darkness, I looked around for _____ *Ind* *something* _____

   to hide behind.

7. Just then, I saw _____ *Ind* *something* _____ with many shining eyes watching

   me from under the bed.

8. I threw _____ *Ref* *myself* _____ in the direction of the light switch.

9. I flipped the switch and found _____ *Ref* *myself* _____ face-to-face with a

   possum and her brood.

10. _____ *Ind* *Nothing* _____ could have prepared me for what I saw next: the

    possum family suddenly appeared to be dead.

11. Thinking of _____ *Ref* *myself* _____ as a murderer, I carried the throw rug

    full of "dead'" possums out to the garden.

12. Later, when I took Mom out to the garden, _____ *Ind* *nothing* _____—not

    one possum—was there.

13. Much later I realized that _____ *Ind* *no one* _____ had ever told me what

    "playing possum" really meant.

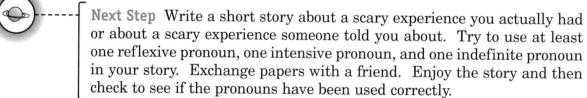

Next Step Write a short story about a scary experience you actually had or about a scary experience someone told you about. Try to use at least one reflexive pronoun, one intensive pronoun, and one indefinite pronoun in your story. Exchange papers with a friend. Enjoy the story and then check to see if the pronouns have been used correctly.

Types of Pronouns 2

Review the special types of pronouns listed below. Notice how each type functions. It might be to ask a question, to point out something, or to relate a subordinate clause to a main clause. (Turn to 444.1-444.3 in *Write Source 2000* for more information.)

EXAMPLES

Interrogative Pronouns:
To *whom* did you give your locker combination?
(An interrogative pronoun asks a question. Use *who, whose,* or *whom* when asking questions about people. Use *which* and *what* when asking about things or ideas.)

Demonstrative Pronouns:
***These* seeds will sprout, but *those* are old and rotten.**
(A demonstrative pronoun points out a thing or an idea without naming it.)
Note: It is incorrect to pair demonstrative pronouns with "here" or "there," such as "This here book . . . ".

Relative Pronouns:
Wolves are not just wild dogs *that* can be easily domesticated.

(*That* refers back to *dogs* and links the underlined subordinate clause to the main clause of the sentence.)

Directions Write a pronoun in the blank in each sentence below. Write *I* above interrogative pronouns, *D* above demonstrative pronouns, and *R* above relative pronouns. The first sentence has been done for you. *Answers will vary.*

1. The sky filled with an eery glow, _____R which_____ we suddenly realized was fire!

2. The mall parking lot was full of snowy mounds, _____R which_____ only an

   hour before had been cars of many shapes and colors.

3. The contractor knows how to select paint _____R that_____ will be durable

   under wet or moist conditions.

4. _____D This/That_____ is a mountain pass that an experienced climber could make,

   but _____D that/this_____ is a deadly crevasse no one could get through.

All Write p. 382

5. A 200-year-old building at Oxford University was saved after its 40-foot

    columns rotted because its original builder, planning ahead, had planted an

    oak grove _____*that*_____ provided the replacement columns.

    (R above "that")

6. _____*What*_____ word game would you like to play?

    (I above "What")

7. Stepping into the jungle _____*that*_____ grew in a thick, thorny tangle,

    (R above "that")

    the inexperienced explorer was instantly lost.

8. _____*That/This*_____ animal is a crocodile, and _____*this/that*_____ is an

    (D above "That/This") *(D above "this/that")*

    alligator.

9. If you had to list the 10 most important inventions of the twentieth century,

    _____*what*_____ would they be?

    (I above "what")

10. The field, _____*which*_____ was still wet from yesterday's rain, turned into

    (R above "which")

    a muddy mess by halftime.

11. Mr. Lawrence, _____*whom*_____ the students secretly nicknamed Lumpy,

    (R above "whom")

    was known for his huge midafternoon snacks.

12. _____*These/Those*_____ cotton jerseys are comfortable, but _____*those/these*_____

    (D above "These/Those") *(D above "those/these")*

    wool ones are scratchy.

13. The coach, _____*whose*_____ job hinged on winning the last two games of

    (R above "whose")

    the season, looked very nervous.

14. _____*Which*_____ country produces more oil, Mexico or Venezuela?

    (I above "Which")

Next Step Find an interesting story in a newspaper. Circle the relative pronouns, underline the demonstrative pronouns, and put brackets around the interrogative pronouns. Before you start, guess which type of pronouns will be used most. Count the circles, underlines, and brackets when you are finished. Was your guess correct?

Pronoun Agreement 1

One of the most important rules of writing is this one: *A pronoun must agree with its antecedent.* Unfortunately, it's also one of the most difficult rules to understand.

Here's what the rule means: Each time you use a pronoun in place of a noun, you must be sure that the pronoun is the same number (singular or plural) and the same person (first, second, third) as the original noun. Clear? Well, maybe the following activity will help to clarify things. (For more information, turn to page 90 and section 441.4 in *Write Source 2000*.)

EXAMPLE

The four *deer* scattered as the skunk approached *them*.
(A pronoun must agree in number with its antecedent. Because the noun *deer* is plural, the pronoun *them* must also be plural.)

Directions   **Cross out the incorrect pronouns in the following sentences. Write corrections above them. The first one has been done for you.**

1. My grandmom rolled her eyes when she heard ~~they~~ *she* can buy eggs laid by

   vegetarian chickens that don't eat bugs or meat by-products.

2. Grandmom always thought eating bugs was good for them.

3. Grandmom says that when she was growing up, kids were expected to eat

   whatever was put in front of ~~you~~ *them*, and so were chickens.

4. "Things change," I said. "When IBM started in the '50s, ~~he~~ *it* thought five

   computers throughout the world would be enough to do the job."

5. My grandmom said ~~her~~ *she* doesn't see what computers have to do with

   chickens.

   All Write pp. 53 and 379

6. I pointed out that computers are used to coordinate the shipping of fruits and

   vegetables, making ~~it~~ *them* available throughout the world any time of the year.

7. Grandmom said we should ask a chicken if ~~they like~~ *it likes* fruits and vegetables

   before we make ~~them~~ *it* eat this food.

8. "Not chickens, Grandmom—people demand special eggs, because ~~he's~~ *they've* gotten

   used to foods from all over the world," I explained.

9. My grandmom says ~~they know~~ *she knows* what ~~they~~ *she* would do if somebody started

   demanding special eggs at ~~their~~ *her* house.

10. Grandmom would plunk that peanut butter jar down on the table and invite

    her guest to make ~~themself~~ *himself or herself* a sandwich.

11. "What if a person eats a special diet for ~~their~~ *his or her* health?" I asked.

12. As long as she doesn't have to cook it, Grandmom supposes a person can eat

    whatever he or she wants.

13. A person should mind ~~their~~ *his or her* manners, Grandmom says.

14. A guest should eat what ~~they're~~ *he or she is* served.

15. People shouldn't make unreasonable demands on the hostess even if it's

    important to stay on ~~her~~ *their* diets.

16. People should thank the cook, Grandmom says, even if ~~him~~ *their* meal is terrible!

Next Step Write a story about something your grandmother or grandfather says (or base your story on a fictional grandmother or grandfather). Try to use a few pronouns in your story. Underline your pronouns and circle their antecedents. Check that the pronouns agree in number and in person with their antecedents.

Pronoun Agreement 2

Do you sometimes need an "antecedent detector"? If you're like most people, you probably wish there was such a gadget—but there's not. You will need to develop your own sense of what makes pronouns and their antecedents clear and easy to read. Rewriting poorly written sentences—like the ones below—will help you develop this sense and, in turn, help you become a better writer. (For more information, see page 90 and 441.4 in your *Write Source 2000* handbook.)

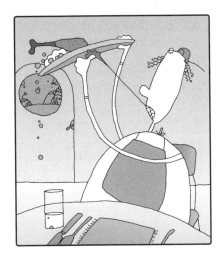

EXAMPLE

Confusing Pronoun Reference:
As I dug into my meal, Karen stuck her gum on my plate, which tasted as good at it looked.

Corrected Sentence:
As Karen stuck her gum on my plate, I dug into my meal, which tasted as good as it looked.

Directions   Find the confusing pronoun references in the sentences below. Then, rewrite each sentence on the lines below it. The first sentence has been done for you.   *Answers will vary.*

1. Most kids appreciate a practical joke, especially if they are a little bit crazy.

   Most kids appreciate a practical joke, especially if it is a little bit crazy.

2. Jack's dad took us for ice cream after the game, while he was bragging about how he made the three-point shot that won the game.

   While Jack was bragging about how he made the three-point shot that

   won the game, his dad took us for ice cream.

3. As I looked out the bedroom window, a doe ran behind our truck, but it moved before I could grab my camera.

   As I looked out the bedroom window, a doe ran behind our truck, but

   she moved before I could grab my camera.

All Write pp. 53 and 379

4. At sunrise in the mountains, the campers were able to ignore their aching muscles and sore feet because they were so beautiful.

Because the mountains were so beautiful at sunrise, the campers

were able to ignore their aching muscles and sore feet.

5. The Scouts had been hiking so long in the mountains that they were worn down.

The Scouts were worn down after they had been hiking so long in the

mountains.

6. Lots of buses stop in front of the school to pick up students, all of them smelling like diesel fuel.

Lots of buses, all of them smelling like diesel fuel, stop in front of

the school to pick up students.

7. I picked up some pretzels when I went for a walk with my dogs, and I ate them.

When I went for a walk with my dogs, I picked up some pretzels, and I

ate them.

8. I helped dry towels with my sisters, hanging them on the clothesline.

I helped my sisters dry towels, hanging them on the clothesline.

_____

Next Step Write down a verse from a song—a traditional song or a song you've heard on the radio. Circle the pronouns. Draw a line from each pronoun to its antecedent. Are all the antecedents clear?

Action and Linking Verbs

I'd saved up for months for my trip to the Super Bowl. The game sizzled. My favorite team won in overtime. But when a reporter asked me what I thought of the game, I could think of only one word: "Awesome!" A few vivid action verbs that afternoon would have saved my big TV moment. Action verbs can also save your writing, turning it from dull to exciting. (Refer to 446.1-446.3 in *Write Source 2000* for more information.)

EXAMPLES

Linking Verbs:
You could *be* a radio programmer and broadcaster.

Action Verbs:
You could *create* and *broadcast* your own radio program.

Directions	Underline the verbs twice in each of the following sentences. (Don't forget to underline helping verbs as well.) Label each action verb with an *A* and each linking verb with an *L*. See page 446 in *Write Source 2000* for a list of linking verbs. The first sentence has been done for you.

1. Some recent movies and television shows *dramatize* **(A)** the danger of asteroids to life on Earth.

2. Some scientists *feel* **(L)** that at least one huge asteroid *smashed* **(A)** into Earth during the time that dinosaurs *roamed* **(A)** the planet.

3. Under the ocean near Mexico's Yucatan Peninsula *lies* **(A)** an impact crater nearly 180 kilometers wide.

4. Scientists *believe* **(A)** an asteroid *crashed* **(A)** there 65 million years ago and *raised* **(A)** a cloud of dust and ash that *cooled* **(A)** Earth and *killed* **(A)** the dinosaurs.

All Write pp. 49 and 383

5. While another asteroid strike like that <u>might</u> not <u>destroy</u> *A* the human race, it
   <u>could</u> <u>wreck</u> *A* our civilization.

6. Asteroids <u>orbit</u> *A* the sun in a "belt" between Mars and Jupiter.

7. Sometimes the gravity of those planets <u>nudges</u> *A* an asteroid out of the belt,
   and it <u>crosses</u> *A* Earth's orbit.

8. Normally Earth's gravity then <u>swings</u> *A* the asteroid further toward the sun,
   where it <u>disintegrates</u> *A*.

9. Earth <u>has</u> *L* several large craters, however, where asteroids <u>have</u> <u>struck</u> *A* in the
   past.

10. Because the moon <u>has</u> *L* no atmosphere, impact craters literally <u>cover</u> *A* its
    surface.

11. Most asteroid strikes <u>happened</u> *A* long, long ago, amid the fury of the solar
    system's formation.

12. In fact, the chance that a major asteroid <u>will</u> <u>strike</u> *A* Earth <u>is</u> *L* very, very
    small.

13. Still, a number of government agencies <u>watch</u> *A* the skies for "killer" asteroids.

14. Even though the chance of a deadly strike <u>is</u> *L* slim, "Better safe than sorry."

Next Step Write a paragraph or two describing an event you witnessed:
a concert, a parade, a game. Use enough action verbs to make your
paragraphs come to life for the reader.

Simple Verb Tenses

A verb does more than express an action or link the subject to another word in a sentence. A verb also expresses tense, or time. A good place to begin a study of verb tenses is with the three simple tenses: **present, past,** and **future.** (Turn to 448.1-448.3 in *Write Source 2000* for more information.)

EXAMPLES

Present Tense:
John <u>walks</u> up to me, his backpack dragging on the ground.

Past Tense:
John <u>walked</u> up to me, his backpack dragging on the ground.

Future Tense:
John <u>will walk</u> up to me, his backpack dragging on the ground.

Directions
Underline the verb twice in each of the following sentences. Then put each sentence in a different "time zone." That is, rewrite each sentence twice, using the verb in all three simple tenses. (Also, underline the verbs with two lines in your new sentences.) The first one has been done for you.

1. **Present:** *My car battery <u>runs</u> down.*

   Past: *My car battery <u>ran</u> down.*

   Future: *My car battery <u>will run</u> down.*

   _____

2. **Present:** *I <u>call</u> the folks at the AAA auto club to help me.*

   _____

   Past: *I <u>called</u> the folks at the AAA auto club to help me.*

   Future: *I <u>will call</u> the folks at the AAA auto club to help me.*

   _____

All Write p. 385

3. Present: _In two minutes flat, the person from AAA starts my car._

Past: _In two minutes flat, the person from AAA started my car._

Future: _In two minutes flat, the person from AAA will start my car._

4. Present: _Mikey balances two dozen paperbacks on his head at once._

Past: _Mikey balanced two dozen paperbacks on his head at once._

Future: _Mikey will balance two dozen paperbacks on his head at once._

5. Present: _The books slide off in all directions._

Past: _The books slid off in all directions._

Future: _The books will slide off in all directions._

6. Present: _The class laughs uproariously._

Past: _The class laughed uproariously._

Future: _The class will laugh uproariously._

Next Step Write one sentence about your last summer. Now put it in present and future tenses. Write one sentence about your next summer. Then rewrite it in past and present tenses.

Perfect Tenses

At times, the action you want to express isn't clearly a present, past, or future action. For example, let's say that you started cleaning your locker five days ago and that you are still cleaning it. Your cleaning is neither a past action nor a present action. Instead, it is an ongoing action. In this type of situation, you need to use one of the three perfect tenses to state the action. Note the use of the perfect tenses in the following sentences. The verb in each sentence is in italics. (Turn to 448.4-448.6 in *Write Source 2000* for more examples.)

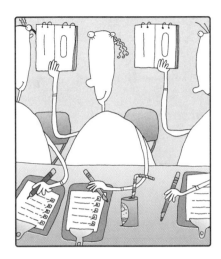

EXAMPLES

Present Perfect Tense:
The amusement park *has remained* my favorite place to spend a summer day.

Past Perfect Tense:
Before this year, the Monster ride *had frightened* me.

Future Perfect Tense:
After this summer, I *will have visited* the park for six straight years.

Directions Using *Write Source 2000*, answer the following questions about the perfect tenses.

1. A verb in the *present perfect tense* expresses action that *began in the past but continues or is completed in the present.*

2. A verb in the *past perfect tense* expresses action that *began in the past and was completed in the past.*

3. A verb in the *future perfect tense* expresses action or existence that *will begin in the future and will be completed by a specific time in the future.*

All Write p. 385

Directions Underline the verb twice in each of these sentences. Don't forget to underline helping verbs as well. In the space provided, label each verb as *present perfect, past perfect,* or *future perfect.* The first one has been done for you.

present perfect **1.** Ned Frap, the ruler of the planet, <u>has escaped</u> in a spacepod.

past perfect **2.** An earthquake <u>had leveled</u> his plastic dome.

future perfect **3.** He <u>will have used</u> all his energy pellets before nightfall.

past perfect **4.** Ned <u>had lived</u> in his dome for six years.

past perfect **5.** In those six years, he <u>had</u> never <u>gone</u> outside.

Directions Underline the verb twice in each of the following sentences. Then rewrite each sentence by changing the verb to the tense indicated in parentheses. Remember that all perfect tenses are composed of a form of *have* plus the past participle of the main verb. The first one has been done for you.

1. The Phantom Blur <u>prepares</u> very carefully for the mission. (**present perfect**)

The Phantom Blur has prepared very carefully for the mission.

2. He <u>sneaks</u> into embassies, castles, and prisons. (**present perfect**)

He has sneaked into embassies, castles, and prisons.

3. Tomorrow, the Phantom Blur <u>will attempt</u> a new mission. (**future perfect**)

Tomorrow, the Phantom Blur will have attempted a new mission.

4. At first, he <u>considered</u> the mission a pushover. (**past perfect**)

At first, he had considered the mission a pushover.

5. Perhaps by tomorrow night he <u>will change</u> his mind. (**future perfect**)

Perhaps by tomorrow night he will have changed his mind.

Next Step Be adventurous, and write about Phantom's next mission in a story. (See "Writing Stories" on pages 183-192 in your *Write Source 2000* handbook for help.) Make sure to use some perfect tenses.

Irregular Verbs

The principal parts of a verb are the **present tense,** the **past tense,** and the **past participle.** While the principal parts of most verbs are simply created by adding "ed" to the main verb (*like, liked, liked*), the different parts of irregular verbs follow no set pattern (*run, ran, run; bite, bit, bitten*). This makes it more challenging to use the principal parts correctly in your writing. This activity—and your handbook—can help. (Turn to page 449 in *Write Source 2000* for a chart of irregular verbs.)

I've seen enough!

Directions A good way to learn these irregular verbs is simply to say them over to yourself several times. They have a certain rhythm that helps to make them stick in your mind. Try these easier ones first. Look at them and say them to yourself several times.

Present Tense	Past Tense	Past Participle
begin	began	begun
bite	bit	bitten
drink	drank	drunk
see	saw	seen
write	wrote	written

Of course, there are many more troublesome verbs, including the following:

bring	brought	brought
burst	burst	burst
drown	drowned	drowned
swing	swung	swung
wake	woke	woken

Directions Now try to fill in the blanks below with the principal parts of the verbs you just studied. Try to do it without looking!

begin	began	begun
drink	drank	drunk
write	wrote	written
swing	swung	swung
drown	drowned	drowned

All Write pp. 387-389

Directions Now turn to the chart of irregular verbs on page 449 in your *Write Source 2000* handbook. Read it slowly to yourself. Listen as a classmate reads it to you. Make note of the verbs that cause you trouble. Study those. Then close your book and fill in the chart that follows. (Check your work when you finish.)

Present Tense	Past Tense	Past Participle
am, be	was, were	been
bite	bit	bitten
bring	brought	brought
catch	caught	caught
come	came	come
do	did	done
draw	drew	drawn
eat	ate	eaten
fall	fell	fallen
fight	fought	fought
fly	flew	flown
know	knew	known
lie (recline)	lay	lain
set	set	set
shake	shook	shaken
swim	swam	swum

Next Step Use the most troublesome verbs (from the list above) in a paragraph. Here's a possible starting point:

I brought a water balloon to the picnic, and it . . .

All Write pp. 388-389

Transitive and Intransitive Verbs

There are two types of action verbs—transitive and intransitive. **Transitive** verbs "transfer" their action to a direct object (and sometimes to an indirect object). The direct object completes the meaning of the sentence, as in the examples that follow. An **intransitive** verb completes its meaning without an object. (See 450.1-450.3 in *Write Source 2000* for more information.)

EXAMPLES

Transitive Verb:

The teacher *handed me* the *extinguisher*.

A **direct object** receives the direct action of the verb. It answers the question *who* or *what* after the verb. The teacher handed me what? (*extinguisher*—direct object)

An **indirect object** is indirectly affected by the verb. It tells *to whom* or *for whom* something is done. The teacher handed the extinguisher to whom? (*me*—indirect object)

Intransitive Verb:

Everyone in our class *walked* quietly down the hall.

An intransitive verb does not need to transfer its action to a direct object to complete the thought. In this sentence, the verb *walked* is intransitive and does not have a direct object.

Directions

Write *T* in front of sentences with transitive verbs and *I* in front of sentences with intransitive verbs. Underline each verb twice; for each transitive verb, circle the direct object. The first one has been done for you.

_T_ **1.** Students sometimes <u>set off</u> fire (alarms) by accident.

_I_ **2.** Yesterday's alarm <u>rang</u> for five minutes.

_T_ **3.** The principal <u>gave</u> specific (instructions) over the P.A.

_T_ **4.** Students and teachers <u>placed</u> their (books) on their desks.

All Write pp. 390-391 and 383

_T_ **5.** Teachers hurriedly <u>ushered</u> (students) into the hall.

_T_ **6.** They <u>counted</u> the (students) as they left the classroom.

_I_ **7.** Out in the hall, smoke <u>poured</u> from the ductwork.

_I_ **8.** Surprisingly, nobody <u>panicked</u>.

_T_ **9.** The students <u>followed</u> (directions) carefully.

_I_ **10.** They <u>filed</u> out to their designated areas.

_T_ **11.** Students <u>had learned</u> good (habits) from previous fire drills.

_I_ **12.** The fire <u>was burning</u> in one of the shop classes.

_T_ **13.** A student <u>had started</u> a (lawn mower) with the gas cap off.

_I_ **14.** Gasoline <u>spilled</u> onto the engine and <u>burst</u> into flames.

_I_ **15.** The fire <u>spread</u> quickly.

_T_ **16.** Some students <u>felt</u> a burning (sensation) in their eyes.

_T_ **17.** They <u>heard</u> (sirens) from the street.

_I_ **18.** A rescue vehicle <u>arrived</u> at the same time as the fire truck.

_I_ **19.** Firefighters <u>hurried</u> into the building.

_I_ **20.** The fire <u>was</u> soon <u>extinguished</u>, but by then most of the school <u>was filled</u> with smoke.

Next Step Some verbs, such as _break, freeze,_ and _sing,_ can be either transitive or intransitive. Choose one of those verbs and write a sentence using it as a transitive verb. Then write another sentence using it as an intransitive verb. Afterward, make a list of at least five more verbs that can be either transitive or intransitive.

Verbals

Verbals have split personalities—they are words that are part verb and part noun or adjective or adverb. For example, add -*ing* to a verb, and it can become a **gerund**—a verb used as a noun. Or add -*ing* or -*ed* to a verb, and it can become a **participle**—a verb used as an adjective. Or introduce a verb with the word *to* and it becomes an **infinitive**—a verb used as either a noun, an adjective, or an adverb. (Turn to 451.1-451.3 in *Write Source 2000* for more information.)

EXAMPLES

Gerund:
Watching an expert play is a good way to improve your game.
(*Watching* is used as a noun and the subject of the sentence.)

Participle:
The cat played a *watching* game with the *confused* mouse.
(*Watching* and *confused* are used as adjectives. *Watching* modifies *game*. *Confused* modifies *mouse.*)

Infinitive:
To watch is to wait.
(*To watch* is the subject and *to wait* is the predicate noun.)

Directions Underline the verbals in the sentences that follow. In the space below the sentence, name the type of verbal you have found, and explain the job it is doing. There may be more than one verbal in each sentence. The first sentence has been done for you.

1. Smirking at a teacher who scolds you is not wise.

    "Smirking" is a gerund used as the subject of the sentence.

2. Rewarding a dog with treats is a good training technique.

    "Rewarding" is a gerund used as the subject of the sentence.

    "Training" is a participle used as an adjective—it modifies "technique."

All Write p. 391

3. Trained elephants perform regularly so that they do not become restless.

"Trained" is a participle used as an adjective—it modifies "elephants."

4. I've always dreamed of acting in a broadway musical.

"Acting" is a gerund used as an object of the preposition "of."

5. I would like to fly like a bird.

"To fly" is an infinitive used as the direct object of the sentence.

6. To win the next three games is the team's goal.

"To win" is an infinitive used as the subject of the sentence.

7. In most sports, timing is everything.

"Timing" is a gerund used as the subject of the sentence.

8. Applying for a passport is a good idea even if you don't have immediate

travel plans.

"Applying" is a gerund used as the subject of the sentence.

Next Step Write three sentences following the direction given for each verbal: (1) Use *laughing* as an adjective, (2) use *walking* as a subject, and (3) use *to play* as a direct object. Now label each verbal as either a gerund, a participle, or an infinitive.

Subject-Verb Agreement 1

The subject and verb of a sentence must agree in number. In other words, if the subject is singular, the verb must be singular, too. If the subject is plural, the verb must be plural. Study the examples below and in *Write Source 2000* before completing the exercise below. (Turn to pages 88-89 and section 446.4 in *Write Source 2000* for more information and examples.)

EXAMPLES

Compound Subjects:

Annie and her roommate are riding to the concert in our van.

(Compound subjects connected by "and" need a plural verb.)

Neither Annie nor her friends are riding home with us.

(With compound subjects connected by "or" or "nor," the verb must agree with the subject nearest to the verb.)

Collective Noun Subjects:

Camp staff report for duty a week before camp begins.

(*Staff* is plural because each member will be coming from a different place.)

This staff is the best group of counselors in Camp Gichagoomie's history.

(The members of the staff are referred to as one group, so the verb is singular.)

Directions   Circle the correct form of the verb in the sentences below. The first sentence has been done for you.

1. A skunk and its enemy *(is, (are))* soon parted.

2. The crew *(eats, (eat))* in groups of four between 11:30 a.m. and 1:30 p.m.

3. Beans and Barley Restaurant *(serve, (serves))* great veggie burgers.

4. Neither the weather nor the traffic *((was,) were)* to blame on the

   afternoon we missed our plane to Los Angeles.

   All Write pp. 51-52 and 387

5. Either math or pre-algebra *(is, are)* a requirement for eighth graders.

6. Congress rarely *(complete, completes)* all the items on the congressional agenda before it adjourns.

7. Cotton candy, carnival rides, and fireworks *(makes, make)* state fairs fun.

8. The Cornhuskers and the Jayhawks *(is, are)* bound to meet in the Big Eight conference play-offs this year.

9. Your mother, father, or legal guardian *(is, are)* required to sign your permission slip.

10. The Summerfest crowd *(was, were)* disbanding when the rain started.

11. Each twin *(faces, face)* unique challenges as one or the other discovers new interests and friends.

12. Neither the faculty nor the students *(is, are)* happy with the change in the schedule.

13. The committee *(has, have)* recommended improvements for school lunches.

14. Buses and bicycles *(shares, share)* the credit for reducing air pollution.

15. The little pig who built his house of bricks claimed that work and play *(doesn't, don't)* mix!

Next Step As a class, talk about examples of subject-verb agreement that seem tricky or confusing. Then write a tricky sentence—possibly similar to one you've discussed. Then write a rule that will help you remember how to figure out whether the verb should be singular or plural in sentences like the one you've composed.

Subject-Verb Agreement 2

Figuring out whether a verb should be singular (to agree with a singular subject) or plural (to agree with a plural subject) can be tricky! Check out the examples and rules on pages 88-89 and in section 446.4 in *Write Source 2000* if you need additional guidance before completing the exercise below.

EXAMPLES

Subject Separated from the Verb:

I myself, not my friends, am responsible for the decisions I make.

(Make sure the subject and verb are in agreement.)

Subject Follows the Verb:

Piled on the table was a week's harvest of beans from Grandma's garden.

(Make sure the "true" subject and the verb agree.)

Indefinite Pronouns:

Everyone needs someone to talk to.

(The following indefinite pronouns require a singular verb: *each, either, neither, one, everyone, anyone, everybody, everything, someone, somebody, anybody, anything, nobody,* and *another*.)

Most of the ghost stories were scary, but none were truly frightening.

(The following indefinite pronouns can be either singular or plural: *all, any, most, none, some*. Check the noun the pronoun stands for to decide whether you need a singular or a plural verb.)

Directions   Circle the correct form of the verb in each sentence below. The first sentence has been done for you.

1. Everyone in a traditional Chinese family (*has,* have) three names, and

   each of those names is written using one character.

2. Each of the characters, which look like pictures, (*stands,* stand) for a

   particular part of the person's name.

All Write pp. 51-52 and 387

3. The family name, followed by the person's given name, *((is,) are)* written first.

4. Some names *(has, (have))* two or three brush strokes, while others have many.

5. A Chinese phone book, quite different from English, Spanish, or German directories, *((lists,) list)* names according to the number of brush strokes in the character representing the family name.

6. The names represented by the simplest characters with only a few brush strokes *(is, (are))* listed near the beginning of the directory.

7. Anyone with a name requiring many brush strokes *((has,) have)* to look for his or her listing near the end of the directory.

8. Everybody who wants to look up friends in the phone book *((has,) have)* to remember more than 3,000 individual characters!

9. Perhaps anyone who grows up learning each word with a picture *((finds,) find)* remembering Chinese characters as easy as remembering how a word sounds.

10. There *(is, (are))* a number of other languages that use characters instead of letters, but Chinese is the most complex.

Next Step If you have problems remembering which indefinite pronouns are singular and which are plural, create a list for each type. Then use the first letters of the pronouns in each list to create an acronym to help you remember them as either singular or plural.

Subject-Verb Agreement 3

Subjects and verbs must agree in number in your sentences. A singular subject needs a singular verb. (The *book is* hidden.) Plural subjects require plural verbs. (The *books are* hidden.) It's also important to know which indefinite pronouns need a singular verb. Pronouns like *each, one,* and *everyone* require singular verbs. (Turn to pages 88-89 and section 446.4 in *Write Source 2000* for more information.)

◉ EXAMPLES

Each of the boys hopes to find a fossil.

Either is capable of finding bones just like paleontologist Othniel Marsh.

Neither Jon nor Sherman expects to find a Brontosaurus bone.

Directions In the following short paragraph, underline the subjects with a single line and their verbs with two lines. The first sentence has been done for you.

1   For a long time, no one realized that the Apatosaurus and the

2   Brontosaurus were the same dinosaur. Different sets of dinosaur bones were

3   found in different places in Wyoming and were thought to be from different

4   dinosaurs. The first skeleton discovered had no skull. The American

5   scientist Othniel Marsh named it Apatosaurus. Two years later, scientists

6   found a more complete skeleton. Marsh named it Brontosaurus. Soon,

7   everyone realized that these two dinosaurs were the same. One of the

8   names—Apatosaurus—has become formally accepted and is used by

9   paleontologists. One of the names—Brontosaurus, the thunder lizard—

10 seems to be more popular with the general public.

All Write pp. 51-52 and 387

Subject-Verb Agreement 4

If the subject of a sentence is separated from its verb by other words or phrases, you may be tempted to make the verb agree with the closest noun—which is not necessarily the subject. One way to avoid this problem is to say the sentence aloud without the words that come between the subject and the verb. Try this technique on the examples below. (Also, turn to pages 88-89 and section 446.4 in *Write Source 2000* for more information.)

EXAMPLES

The <u>raptors</u> in the time of dinosaurs <u>were</u> fast and able hunters.

Fossil <u>eggs</u> found in the desert <u>prove</u> dinosaur mothers put their eggs in nests.

Directions Read the sentences below. Then rewrite the sentences, separating the subject and the verb with a phrase. The first one has been done for you. *Answers will vary.*

1. <u>Raptors</u> <u>were</u> hungry all the time.

   Raptors feeding on small animals were hungry all the time.

2. <u>Dinosaurs</u> <u>lived</u> millions of years ago.

   _____

   _____

3. <u>Fossils</u> <u>tell</u> us about dinosaurs.

   _____

4. Some <u>dinosaurs</u> <u>were</u> bigger than houses.

   _____

   _____

5. <u>Tyrannosaurus Rex</u> <u>was</u> the biggest meat eater.

   _____

   _____

Types of Adjectives

There are four special kinds of adjectives. They are compound, demonstrative, indefinite, and predicate. (Turn to sections 452.2-452.5 in *Write Source 2000* for help with this exercise.)

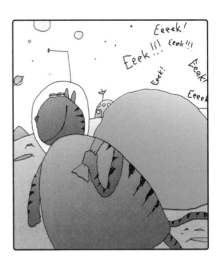

Directions   Each sentence has a different type of adjective underlined. In the space beneath each sentence, identify and then provide an explanation for each type.

1. <u>Some</u> cats enjoy having <u>many</u> mice around.

Type: _Indefinite Adjectives_

Explanation: An _____indefinite_____ adjective is one that _gives an_ _approximate number or quantity._

2. <u>This</u> kitten is mean, but <u>that</u> cat is meaner.

Type: _Demonstrative Adjectives_

Explanation: _A demonstrative adjective is one that points out a particular noun._

3. <u>Scar-faced</u> Bronty is no <u>scaredy-cat</u> guard.

Type: _Compound Adjectives_

Explanation: _A compound adjective is made up of more than one word. (Sometimes it is hyphenated.)_

4. A frustrated kitten is <u>unpleasant</u> and <u>unpredictable</u>.

Type: _Predicate Adjectives_

Explanation: _A predicate adjective is an adjective that follows a linking verb and describes the subject._

    All Write p. 394

Directions Use one of the four types of adjectives as one of the central characters in a story. An indefinite adjective, for example, might only think or speak in very general terms. Its favorite phrase might be "Gee, I'm not sure." A demonstrative adjective, on the other hand, might be very bossy. (Ask your teacher if you may work in pairs for this activity.)

_____

_____

_____

_____

_____

_____

_____

_____

_____

_____

_____

_____

_____

_____

_____

_____

Next Step Share your stories in your writing groups or with your class as a whole. Pay special attention to each adjective's personality.

Compound Adjectives

The screen door slams. Three-year-old Pooki runs into the kitchen and rummages through cabinets, asking, "Where is my zoo-buggy house?"

I hand my little neighbor the screen-topped "bug zoo" we made for catching fireflies. Pooki combines simple words she knows into picture-perfect descriptions without batting an eye.

Compound adjectives—two simple words linked as one compound word—are fun to use and, in informal writing, fun to invent. (Turn to section 452.3 in *Write Source 2000* for more information.)

EXAMPLES

The fun-loving friends played kickball at the park.
(*Kickball* always appears as one word; *fun-loving* doesn't.)

five-dollar bill   second-story office   40-something years
(Numbers combined with words to form compound adjectives are hyphenated.)

The old sock collector paid 50 dollars for hand-knitted argyles.
(Was the collector old? Then write old sock-collector. Or was he a collector of old socks? If so, write old-sock collector.)

| Directions | Write compound adjectives in the blanks below. The first blank has been done for you. If you need help thinking of compound words, check out the word bank on the next page. |

Answers may vary.

1   I will never forget the crazy, _____*goofed-up*_____ Halloween party my

2   sister and I threw for our _____*eighth-grade*_____ friends. When the

3   _____*30-some*_____ kids started arriving around 6:00 p.m., things

4   looked normal. Within hours, though, everything changed.

5   We had the party in our _____*cleaned-up*_____ barn. There was just one

6   _____*teeny-weeny*_____ problem: my sister's _____*bullheaded*_____ donkey.

      All Write p. 394

7   George, the donkey, doesn't move out of his _____*straw-stuffed*_____ stall

8 unless it is his idea. So our _____*half-baked*_____ plan was to include him in

9 the party. George would be a steed in _____*tinfoil*_____ armor. Instead of

10 bobbing for apples, our _____*fun-loving*_____ guests would hop on George and

11 ride toward a _____*pumpkin-head*_____ scarecrow. The winner would have to knock

12 the scarecrow's _____*oversized*_____ head off with a _____*lambs-wool*_____

13 duster. It sounded simple.

14   We didn't anticipate George's _____*so-called*_____ enthusiasm for acting.

15 Instead of aiming for the scarecrow, George headed for the _____*well-decorated*_____

16 refreshment table. As he slammed into the sawhorses supporting the

17 tabletop, soda pop cans burst and sprayed sticky fountains at the

18 _____*overhead*_____ lights. The lights went out.

19   Shrieking kids crowded toward the door of the _____*blacked-out*_____

20 barn. There, they ran smack into a _____*snaggletoothed*_____ phantom with

21 burning eyes! Was it a _____*fire-breathing*_____ monster? Nope. It was our

22 _____*lawn-mower*_____ tractor covered with _____*glow-in-the-dark*_____ paint!

goofed-up	happy-go-lucky	bullheaded	straw-stuffed	blacked-out
glow-in-the-dark	eighth-grade	30-some	cleaned-up	fire-breathing
overhead	so-called	pumpkin-head	makeshift	teeny-weeny
lawn-mower	well-decorated	tinfoil	lambs-wool	warm-up
snaggletoothed	oversized	half-baked	fun-loving	noise-making

Predicate Adjectives

You know that an adjective tells something special about a noun. The noun a predicate adjective describes is always the subject of a sentence or a clause. Predicate adjectives are easy to spot, too, because they always follow a linking verb.

"Wait a minute," you're thinking. "Predicate nouns follow linking verbs, too!" Indeed, they do—but predicate nouns rename the subject instead of describing it. (Turn to 441.1 and 452.5 in *Write Source 2000* for more information.)

EXAMPLES

Predicate Adjective:

The <u>future</u> <u>is</u> *predictable* in science fiction.

(The verb *is* links the subject noun *future* to its predicate adjective *predictable*.)

Predicate Noun:

<u>Aliens</u> <u>is</u> a science-fiction *movie* about the future.

(The verb *is* links the subject *Aliens* to the predicate noun *movie*.)

Note: Most **linking verbs** are forms of the verb *be—am, is, are, was, were, be, being, been.* Other verbs—*smell, feel, look, taste, remain, appear, sound, seem, become, grow, stand,* and *turn*—may also do the job of linking a subject to a predicate noun or a predicate adjective. Some words may be used as both linking verbs and action verbs. How the verb functions in a *particular* sentence is the key to whether it is a linking verb or an action verb.

| Directions | In the sentences below, underline the subject once and the verb twice. Then label each bold-faced word: *PA* for predicate adjective or *PN* for predicate noun. The first one has been done for you. |

1. <u>People</u> <u>are</u> **curious** about finding new ways to build houses.
   [PA above **curious**]

2. A <u>house</u> <u>may</u> not <u>look</u> any **different** from its neighbor, but its building <u>blocks</u>
   [PA above **different**]
   <u>may be</u> **revolutionary!**
   [PA above **revolutionary**]

3. Straw-bale <u>houses</u> <u>are</u> magnificent **estates** or simple **huts.**
   [PN above **estates**] [PN above **huts**]

All Write pp. 378 and 394

4. The laziest one of the *Three Little Pigs* was not the first **builder** *[PN]* to decide that straw is an excellent construction **material** *[PN]*.

5. Houses of compacted straw coated with clay were **common** *[PA]* in ancient Asia and Europe.

6. A one-room schoolhouse built in 1886 near Bayard, Nebraska, is the first documented **building** *[PN]* made of rectangular bales.

7. An article in a book titled *Shelter* is **responsible** *[PA]* for renewed interest in straw-bale building.

8. Straw houses coated with stucco, plaster, or clay look **beautiful** *[PA]* and are very **durable** *[PA]*.

9. The houses are unusually **well-insulated** *[PA]*.

10. Straw is an abundant and a renewable **resource** *[PN]*.

11. Air in a straw house is generally **free** *[PA]* of fumes and pollutants.

12. Building with bales is **speedy** *[PA]*; walls can be erected in one weekend.

13. Houses built of straw are still **rare** *[PA]*—but they can be found from the United States to Russia, and from France to Nova Scotia and Mexico.

Next Step Read about other unusual kinds of houses in other books at your library. Let your imagination run wild! Write a description of your ideal house in your journal. Use some colorful predicate adjectives.

Forms of Adjectives

An adjective is used to describe a noun or a pronoun—"the *small* ball." An adjective can even go a step further when it is used in a comparison—"the ball is *smaller* than your fist." Each adjective has three forms of comparison: *positive, comparative,* and *superlative.* (See the examples below and sections 453.1-453.6 in your *Write Source 2000* handbook for more information.)

EXAMPLES

Positive:

Frozen yogurt is a *light* dessert. It is *delicious*.
(The *positive form* of an adjective describes a noun or a pronoun without comparing it to anyone or anything else.)

Comparative:

Frozen yogurt is a *lighter* dessert than ice cream.

Frozen yogurt is *more delicious* than ice cream.
(The *comparative form* of an adjective [adjective + *er*] compares two nouns or pronouns. Most adjectives of two or more syllables use the modifier *more,* instead of adding *-er,* to show the comparison.)

Superlative:

Frozen yogurt is the *lightest* dessert of the five on this menu.

Frozen yogurt is the *most delicious* dessert I can think of.
(The *superlative form* of an adjective [adjective + *est*] compares three or more nouns or pronouns. Most adjectives of two or more syllables use the modifier *most,* instead of adding *-est,* to show the comparison.)

Note: A few adjectives are irregular (*good, better, best* and *little, less, least*).

Directions	Use each of the following adjectives in a sentence. Use the adjective in the form indicated in parentheses. The first one has been done for you.

tall **1.** At 20,320 feet, Mt. McKinley is _____*tall*_____ , while South
(positive)

America's Mt. Aconcagua is even _____*taller*_____ , but Mt.
(comparative)

Everest is the _____*tallest*_____ .
(superlative)

All Write p. 395

old   **2.** Evan, born at 11:59 p.m. on July 3, is a day ___*older*___ than
                   (comparative)

his twin brother, born at 12:04 a.m. on July 4.

funny   **3.** Who is the ___*funniest*___ comedian on television?
            (superlative)

good   **4.** I am good at all of the "extreme-B" sports—boards, blades, and

BMX biking—but I am ___*best*___ at snowboarding.
               (superlative)

charming   **5.** The only quality my mom finds ___*more charming*___ in a
                     (comparative)

daughter than whining is the ability to burp on command.

good   **6.** You can buy many types of tires for a road bike, but for traction

on dry pavement, the ___*best*___ tire has no tread, so its
               (superlative)

surface is totally in contact with the road.

comfortable   **7.** My dad's recliner is really ugly, but it is ___*more comfortable*___
                     (comparative)

than my mom's rocking chair.

boring   **8.** That picnic was so ___*boring*___ that even the mosquitoes
            (positive)

fell asleep, but it was not the ___*most boring*___ picnic I've
                 (superlative)

ever attended.

bad   **9.** My brother got a ___*bad*___ grade in ninth-grade
            (positive)

algebra, but my grade was ___*worse*___ .
            (comparative)

Next Step As you completed the activity above, you probably noticed that some adjectives like *bad, worse,* and *worst* are irregular. Compare notes with your classmates and see how many irregular adjectives you can think of.

Adverbs

Adverbs are used to modify verbs, adjectives, or other adverbs. There are four basic types of adverbs: *adverbs of time, place, manner,* and *degree.* (Turn to 454.2 in *Write Source 2000* for more information.)

Directions Circle 11 adverbs in the following sentences. The first sentence has been done for you.

1. Lightning streaked (continuously,) driving jagged spears into the dark night.

2. John's mother (hesitantly) and (shakily) agreed that the lightning was pretty.

3. Four-year-old John found the whole experience (quite) exciting.

4. (Suddenly,) they were plunged into darkness.

5. To move in the dark was (very) difficult, but they (slowly) managed to find their way.

6. The first thing that they spotted was a (brightly) flashing red light.

7. Cars were moving (slowly) as they approached the corner.

8. John and his mother walked (cautiously) across the street.

9. They stepped (carefully) onto the curb.

10. John and his mother will (never) forget that experience.

Next Step Write four more adverbs on the lines below. Then use all five adverbs in sentences in a very short story.

especially _____ _____

_____ _____ _____

All Write p. 396

Directions   In the space below, write a descriptive paragraph about drivers of cars or motorcycles and how they maneuver through traffic. Use each of the listed adverbs in the paragraph. (See pages 100 and 454 in *Write Source 2000*.)

well   fast   quickly   often   entirely

_____

_____

_____

_____

_____

_____

_____

_____

_____

_____

_____

_____

_____

_____

_____

_____

_____

All Write pp. 62 and 396

Forms of Adverbs

An adverb is a word that tells us more about a verb, an adjective, or another adverb. Adverbs usually explain *how, when, where,* or *to what extent (how often, how long, how much)* something happened.

They have three forms: positive, comparative, and superlative. The positive form modifies another word without making a comparison. (Turn to section 454.1 in *Write Source 2000* for more information.)

EXAMPLES

Positive:
Performing fleas train *vigorously*.
(*Vigorously* modifies the verb *train* without making any comparisons.)

Comparative:
Jumping frogs train *more vigorously* than performing fleas.
(*More vigorously* modifies the verb *train* and compares how *frogs* train to how *fleas* train.)

Superlative:
Fido's flea is the *most vigorously* trained insect in the world.
(*Most vigorously* modifies the adjective *trained* and compares one *flea* to all other insects.)

Directions Use each of the following words as an adverb in a sentence. (Use the adverb in the form indicated in parentheses.) The first one has been done for you.

bad **1.** When the teacher stepped out of the room, the students behaved
____*badly*____ .
(positive)

clear **2.** Greg speaks ____*more clearly*____ than Ann, his opponent
(comparative)
for student counsel.

fast **3.** Who ran ____*fastest*____ in the relay?
(superlative)

gentle **4.** She ____*gently*____ stroked the frightened dog.
(positive)

All Write p. 397

noisy **5.** Mark my words, this discussion began quietly, but it will end

_____noisily_____ .
(positive)

careful **6.** Lock the door _____carefully_____ — _____more carefully_____
(positive)   (comparative)

than you have ever done it before!

loud **7.** Marshmallow Man from *Ghostbusters* stomps around

_____loudly_____ .
(positive)

quick **8.** He won the pancake-eating contest by floating the flapjacks in

milk and gulping them _____most quickly_____ .
(superlative)

sincere **9.** Think carefully about the questions, and answer them

_____sincerely_____ .
(positive)

stylish **10.** The '57 Thunderbird sports car was designed _____more stylishly_____
(comparative)

than that year's Chevy model, but the Chevy has become a legend.

well **11.** Picabo Street skied _____best_____ in the 1998 Winter Olympics,
(superlative)

even though she was recovering from a serious injury.

slow **12.** Please drive _slow (or slowly)_ !
(positive)

Next Step Now you try it! Write three sentences about a game or contest. Write one sentence in which you use one adverb in the positive form, one in the comparative form, and one in the superlative form.

Double Negatives and Incorrect Usage

This is a test. This is o

As you talk with your friends, you'll probably hear a lot of *nonstandard language*. What is natural in spoken language can be confusing in written communication.

Though double negatives are common in song lyrics and casual speech, you should avoid them when writing, unless you are quoting someone or creating an informal sentence. (Turn to page 91 in *Write Source 2000* for more information.)

EXAMPLES

Incorrect:
We don't need no money.
(Does this mean "We don't need money" or "We need money"?)

Correct:
We don't need any money.
(The meaning—"We don't need money"—is clear.)

Incorrect:
I didn't barely pass the test.
(Does this sentence mean "I did pass"? Or does it mean "I didn't pass"?)

Correct:
I barely passed the test.
(The meaning—"I barely passed the test"—is clear.)

Note: Do not use *hardly, barely,* or *scarcely* with a negative word; the result is a double negative.

Directions   Circle the correct negative for each sentence below. The first one has been done for you.

1. There *(isn't hardly no,* (*is hardly any*)) time to practice before our first soccer game.

2. Chocolate can poison canines, so be careful never to give ((*any,*) *none*) to your dog.

    All Write p. 54

3. We don't need *(no, any)* heroes—just a few true friends.

4. Antarctica doesn't have *(none, any)* of the food plants of other climes.

5. Antarctica's ice contains tiny algae that *(aren't no, are no)* bigger than a single cell.

6. Shrimplike organisms called krill, *(scarcely no bigger, scarcely bigger)* than the algae, eat the single-celled plants, becoming part of the food chain that supports whales, penguins, and seals.

7. I can't think of *(nothing, anything)* better than living on a houseboat.

8. Our parrot doesn't say *(no, any)* words, but he mimics the sounds of our dishwasher, our telephone, and the family cat!

9. Aaron didn't have *(no, any)* money for a boat, so he made a raft by tying empty milk jugs to a couple of old doors.

10. Scarcely *(nobody, anybody)* showed up to audition for a part in our school's production of *Our Town*.

11. Later that year, so many people tried out for *West Side Story* that we *(couldn't hardly, could hardly)* all cram into the practice gym.

12. Ann didn't want *(no, any)* part of Jake's plan to put sea monkeys in Miss Han's classroom aquarium.

Next Step Collect several examples of standard and nonstandard language from magazines, TV, and the radio. Jot them down on a sheet of paper. Explain why each example is an appropriate (or inappropriate) piece for its intended audience and purpose.

Prepositions

Prepositions such as *at, about, by, for, in, of, on,* and *to,* among others, have been used in our language for well over 1,400 years. Prepositions are words that show position or direction. They also introduce prepositional phrases.

Prepositional phrases are an indispensable part of our language. (*Indispensable* means we can't do without them.) Just think how sentences, such as the examples below, would read without the prepositional phrases. There wouldn't be much left, would there? (Turn to 455.1-455.3 in *Write Source 2000* for more information.)

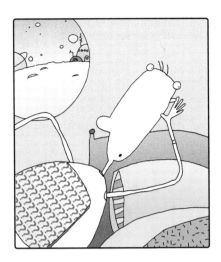

EXAMPLES

Prepositional Phrases:

Write every day *in a personal journal*.

Begin writing *with a particular idea in mind*.

| Directions | Underline all of the prepositional phrases in the journal entry below. *Caution:* Do not underline infinitives as prepositional phrases! The first one has been done for you. |

1   April 12

2   I was late <u>for my guitar lesson</u> tonight. Usually, I'm <u>at the studio</u>

3   <u>by 6:30</u>, but I was late <u>because of my cat Tom</u>. He ran away

4   <u>during last night's storm</u>. I looked everywhere <u>for him</u>.

5   I looked <u>in the garage</u> because there are lots <u>of little niches</u> <u>in there</u>.

6   I looked <u>in the laundry room</u> because cats usually like to curl up

7   <u>in warm, soft places</u>. I finally headed outside and even looked <u>in the trees</u>.

8   Tom just wasn't to be found, so I stopped looking. <u>After supper</u>, I heard a

9   purr <u>in my room</u>. Leave it <u>to a cat</u> to be unpredictable. I found Tom

10 <u>under the bed</u>.

All Write p. 398

| **Directions** | Rewrite the following sentences so that each begins with a prepositional phrase. Place a comma after the phrase if you think one is needed to make the meaning of the sentence clear. The first one has been done for you. |

1. Dogs are often used as companions in modern nursing homes.

   In modern nursing homes, dogs are often used as companions.

2. Many people in nursing homes think of the resident dog as their very own pet.

   In nursing homes, many of the people think of the resident dog as

   their very own pet.

3. Some residents leave out special treats for the dog's daily visit.

   For the dog's daily visit, some residents leave out special treats.

4. Golden retrievers are suitable pets according to some staff members.

   According to some staff members, golden retrievers are suitable

   pets.

5. The nurses usually walk the dogs between shifts.

   Between shifts, the nurses usually walk the dogs.

Next Step Write a story starter, similar to the one below, using a two-word preposition from the list at 455.3 in your *Write Source 2000* handbook. (Share your results.)

Together with her friend, Elisha was a curious young lady.
One foggy September evening, her curiosity led to . . .

Interjections

An interjection is a word or phrase used to express strong emotion or surprise. Wow! and Yikes! are interjections. A comma or an exclamation point is usually used to separate the interjection from the rest of the sentence. (Turn to page 453 in *Write Source 2000* for more information.)

Directions	Underline each interjection in the sentences that follow. The first one has been done for you.

1. "Hey, Joe, guess where I'm going next week?"

2. "Well, let's see," answered Joe. "To Australia? Siberia? The Moon?"

3. "Okay, enough of the wise-guy routine. I'm going scuba diving."

4. "Cool. Do you get to use air tanks and all that?" asked Joe.

5. "Yep, and we get to explore a coral reef and a couple of shipwrecks."

6. "Holy mackerel! That sounds like a great time. Do you need someone to carry your flippers or something?" asked Joe, drooling.

7. "Oops, I forgot to sign up for flippers. Thanks for reminding me."

8. "What kind of creatures do you expect to see? I mean, whoa, you better stay away from the sharks, barracudas, and octopuses," warned Joe.

9. "Yeah, I'll keep my distance. Hmmm, maybe I should buy some shark repellent or something."

10. "Nah," Joe laughed. "No shark is going to be interested in someone as tasteless as you!"

All Write p. 397

Directions

On the lines below, write your own dialogue about an adventure you've had (or would like to have). Use interjections whenever they seem right. If they are used well, interjections will make your dialogue sound much more real.

_____

_____

_____

_____

_____

_____

_____

_____

_____

_____

_____

_____

_____

_____

_____

_____

_____

_____

_____

Subordinating Conjunctions

Subordinating conjunctions connect clauses to form complex sentences. The resulting complex sentences often carry more meaning than the shorter independent clauses and also help to make your writing read more smoothly. (Turn to 456.3-456.4 in *Write Source 2000* for more information.)

EXAMPLES

Two Sentences:

Martha entered a 124-mile ice-skating race. She felt ready for it.

A Compound Sentence:

Martha entered a 124-mile ice-skating race, and she felt ready for it.
(A comma and the coordinating conjunction *and* connect the two sentences.)

A Complex Sentence:

Martha entered a 124-mile ice-skating race because she felt ready for it.
(The subordinating conjunction *because* connects the two sentences.)

| Directions | Subordinating conjunctions connect two ideas to form meaningful complex sentences. Some subordinating conjunctions express time *(before)*, some express the reason why *(because)*, and some serve as conditional words *(unless)*. In each of the sentences, circle the subordinating conjunctions. Put the group of words (or clause) each conjunction introduces in parentheses. The first one has been done for you. |

1. For his own safety, a soccer referee in Greece disguised himself as a priest after a match (because) (he had greatly upset the local fans).

2. Alex Wickham must have had a lot of confidence (since) (he dove from a rocky cliff the height of a 20-story building).

3. He lost consciousness (before) (he hit the water).

4. (Although) (he survived the dive), his body was all black-and-blue.

All Write p. 399

5. Two tennis players once continued a point for 78 straight minutes (until) (one player had to stop the volley to give a tennis lesson).

6. (When) (Lawson Robertson and Harry Hillman set a track-and-field record) they did it in a three-legged race.

7. (Although) (he had a 150-pound man on his back) Noah Young ran a mile in 8 minutes 30 seconds.

8. (While) (Ernest Mensen ran a distance of 1,960 miles) he ate only biscuits covered with raspberry syrup.

9. Ernest Mensen saved time (when) (he ran) (because) (he knew how to find shortcuts through forests)

10. The modern marathon race got its name from the plain of Marathon in Greece (where) (an ancient battle took place).

11. (When) (a man named Philippedes ran from Marathon to Athens) he delivered the news of a Greek victory over Persia.

12. (Because) (the first marathon was 26 miles) the modern marathon race during the Olympic Games is also 26 miles.

Next Step Write a paragraph about a cooking, camping, or classroom experience. Use short, simple sentences as if you were just learning to read and write. Then exchange paragraphs with a classmate and revise each other's work. Try to use some subordinate conjunctions in your revisions.

Coordinating and Correlative Conjunctions

The place two roads come together is called a *junction*. A similar word *conjunction* is the name of the part of speech that joins things—other words, phrases, or clauses. There are three types of conjunctions. This exercise will look at two of the three types: coordinating and correlative. **Coordinating conjunctions** always connect two equal sentence elements of the same kind—a word to a word, a phrase to a phrase, or a clause to a clause. **Correlative conjunctions,** like coordinating conjunctions, connect elements of the same kind, but correlative conjunctions are used in pairs. (Turn to 456.1-456.2 and 456.4 in *Write Source 2000* for more information.)

EXAMPLES

Coordinating Conjunction:
Mathematics *and* music communicate without language.
(The coordinating conjunction *and* connects two words—*mathematics* and *music*.)

Correlative Conjunction:
Choose *either* music *or* art as your elective class.
(The correlative conjunctions *either, or* connect two words—*music* and *art*.)

Directions	Join each pair of sentences that follow using coordinating or correlative conjunctions. You may delete words and move words around. The first sentence has been done for you.

Answers may vary.

1. I would like to visit Iceland. I would also like to visit Greenland.

   I would like to visit Iceland and Greenland.

2. In high school, I want to try out for track. I also want to try out for basketball.

   In high school, I want to try out for track and basketball.

   _____

3. Many athletes want to play two sports. The seasons have to be at different times.

   Many athletes want to play two sports, but the seasons have to be at

   different times.

All Write pp. 316 and 399

4. In some places football and soccer have the same season. A student must choose one sport or the other.

In some places football and soccer have the same season, so a

student must choose one sport or the other.

5. My brother could not decide which sport to play. He had to choose football or soccer.

My brother could not decide whether to play football or to play soccer.

6. He enjoys both sports. He's pretty good at football and soccer.

He enjoys both football and soccer, and he's pretty good at both

sports.

7. He finally chose football. He was happy to have made a decision.

He finally chose football and was happy to have made a decision.

8. He was unhappy about missing his friends on the soccer team. He also thought he would miss the constant movement and pace of a soccer game.

He was unhappy not only about missing his friends on the soccer

team but also about missing the constant movement and pace of

a soccer game.

9. Now he talks about football all the time. We used to talk together about both soccer and football.

We used to talk together about both soccer and football, but now he

talks about football all the time.

Parts of Speech Review 1

In the English language there are eight parts of speech. They help you understand words and how to use them. Every word in every sentence is a part of speech.

Directions Name one of the eight parts of speech for each of the eight "bright, shiny faces." Don't look in your *Write Source 2000* handbook (at least, not yet), but rather, try to name all of them on your own. Then, if the "inkwell" runs dry and you can't think of any more, turn to page 457 in your handbook.

noun   conjunction   preposition   pronoun

adjective   *verb*   *adverb*   *interjection*

All Write p. 374

Directions	Pair up with a classmate and, as a team, identify the part of speech for each underlined word. There are five examples of each part of speech, except for the interjection, which has only one example. (Look at pages 439-457 in *Write Source 2000*.)

                                                           verb   preposition

1   In the summer after eighth grade, Rene <u>took</u> a bus <u>from</u> Vermont to
                                                     adjective

2   her uncle's cottage in New Jersey. Her "<u>graduation</u> present" turned out to be
    adjective

3   a <u>crash</u> course in the school of life.
                          noun   *adverb*

4   At a stop in <u>New York City</u>, she visited a newsstand. <u>Suddenly</u>, someone
                       adverb   *conjunction*

5   snatched her purse. She <u>never</u> saw the thief. Her ticket <u>and</u> her money were
                        conjunction   *verb*

6   gone. She patted her side <u>as if</u> the bag would reappear. Anger <u>overwhelmed</u>
   interjection   *pronoun*   *preposition*

7   her. <u>Oh</u>, how could <u>someone</u> be so evil? How would she get <u>to</u> Ocean City now?
                                    pronoun   *preposition*

8   Fortunately, the bus driver let her call her parents. <u>They</u> told her <u>about</u>
                        adjective

9   Western Union, the <u>nationwide</u> telegraph network. Her parents promised to
                        noun

10 wire money to the nearest <u>agent</u>.
               preposition   *verb   pronoun*

11   Hiking <u>through</u> downtown Manhattan, she <u>composed</u> <u>herself</u>. In high
            verb   *adjective*

12 school, she <u>would</u> write a fine story about her adventure. In the <u>cramped</u>
                             preposition   *noun*

13 Western Union office, she studied people <u>with</u> a writer's <u>eye</u>. They looked
 adjective   *pronoun*   *verb*   *noun*   *conjunction*

14 <u>tired</u> and afraid. <u>Everyone</u> there <u>had</u> a <u>problem</u>. But <u>when</u> a man beside her

15 in a tie-dyed T-shirt started to whistle, everybody laughed. They became a

16 kind of family.
        adverb conjunction

17   <u>Later</u>, <u>while</u> she was sunning herself on the Jersey shore, she decided
                 adverb   *noun   conjunction*

18 her story would <u>not</u> be about crime. It would be about the <u>feelings</u> <u>and</u>
            pronoun   *adverb*

19 experiences <u>that</u> draw people <u>together</u>.

       Next Step Write your own sentences with examples of the different parts of speech underlined. Exchange your sentences with a classmate.

All Write pp. 374-399

Parts of Speech Review 2

Directions   Do you know all eight parts of speech? Unscramble the words below to refresh your memory. Then tackle the exercise, identifying the part of speech for each underlined word. The number after each scrambled word tells you how many examples of that part of speech are underlined in the exercise. A few words have been labeled for you. (See pages 439-457 in your handbook.)

1. unno   _noun_ (6)   5. tadviejec   _adjective_ (6)

2. berv   _verb_ (6)   6. brevda   _adverb_ (6)

3. spotiperion   _preposition_ (6) 7. junconontic   _conjunction_ (6)

4. ropnoun   _pronoun_ (6)   8. jecretnition   _interjection_ (1)

1   You would <u>recognize</u> *[verb]* Robin Williams or Danny DeVito <u>on</u> *[preposition]* TV. But

2 would you recognize a picture of the most <u>famous</u> *[adjective]* cartoon-voice actor in

3 history, the man who created over 500 different voices?

4   The man <u>with</u> *[preposition]* the rubber voice was <u>Mel Blanc</u> *[noun]*. You <u>know</u> *[verb]* him as Bugs

5 Bunny and Foghorn Leghorn, as Yosemite Sam <u>and</u> *[conjunction]* the Tasmanian Devil, as

6 Fred Flintstone and Porky Pig—to name just a few of the hundreds of

7 <u>characters</u> *[noun]* he created <u>for</u> *[preposition]* Warner Brothers. During the glory days of radio,

8 Blanc performed <u>weekly</u> *[adverb]* in 18 transcontinental radio shows. He also

9 <u>commanded</u> *[verb]* top pay when recording for <u>rival</u> *[adjective]* companies, once earning $800

10 for Gideon the Cat's hiccup in the Disney movie *Pinocchio*. (At the time,

11 other cartoon actors were earning a mere $50 a day.)

12   Blanc started his <u>career</u> *[noun]* as a musician and bandleader. <u>Luckily</u> *[adverb]* for <u>us</u> *[pronoun]*,

13 one evening in the 1930s he was asked to host a talent show in Portland,

All Write pp. 374-399

14   Oregon. A blizzard forced the contestants to stay home.

                                                           pronoun   *adverb*
15   Blanc decided to do the entire show <u>himself</u>! He <u>cleverly</u> created a

16   voice for each of the "contestants"—a yodeler, a violinist, and a hillbilly—

                                           pronoun   *adjective*
17   and faked interviews with <u>them</u>, using his "<u>real</u>" voice as the interviewer.

18   The audience loved him.

19   After his surprising success, Blanc headed for Hollywood. Getting an
        preposition
20   audition <u>with</u> a cartoon company was not easy. For a year and a half,

                                                         noun   *conjunction*
21   Warner Brothers refused to hear him. His lucky <u>break</u> came <u>when</u> the
           verb
22   studio <u>needed</u> a new voice for a drunken bull.

23   About that time, Warner Brothers was developing the character of a
   adjective   *conjunction*
24   <u>timid</u> little pig. When Blanc was asked in a interview <u>if</u> he had lived on a
                verb *interjection*   *conjunction*
25   farm, he <u>replied</u>, "<u>No</u>, but I went out to a pig farm <u>and</u> wallowed around for
                                        pronoun
26   a couple of weeks." <u>That</u> is how Porky Pig got his voice.
        preposition
27   <u>Around</u> that time, Bugs Hardaway was developing another new
                pronoun
28   character. <u>He</u> described Happy Rabbit as little, tough, and a real stinker.
                adverb   *adjective*
29   Mel Blanc <u>thoughtfully</u> remarked that the <u>toughest</u> voice in the United
                                noun   *adverb*
30   States had to be from the <u>Bronx</u> or Brooklyn. Blanc <u>easily</u> combined the
                noun
31   New York <u>accents</u> and then suggested that Happy Rabbit's name should be

32   changed to honor his creator. Thus, Bugs Bunny was born.
                                adverb   *conjunction*
33   Sylvester the Cat got a <u>very</u> slurpy sounding voice <u>because</u> he is a
   adjective   *conjunction*
34   <u>sloppy-looking</u> cat. Daffy Duck's voice is a lot like Sylvester's <u>but</u> was
                preposition
35   recorded <u>at</u> a different speed. Because he is tiny, Tweety got a baby voice.
                                pronoun   *verb*
36   Even Woody Woodpecker, <u>who</u> was performed by Walter Lanz, <u>owes</u> his

37   trademark laugh to Mel Blanc.